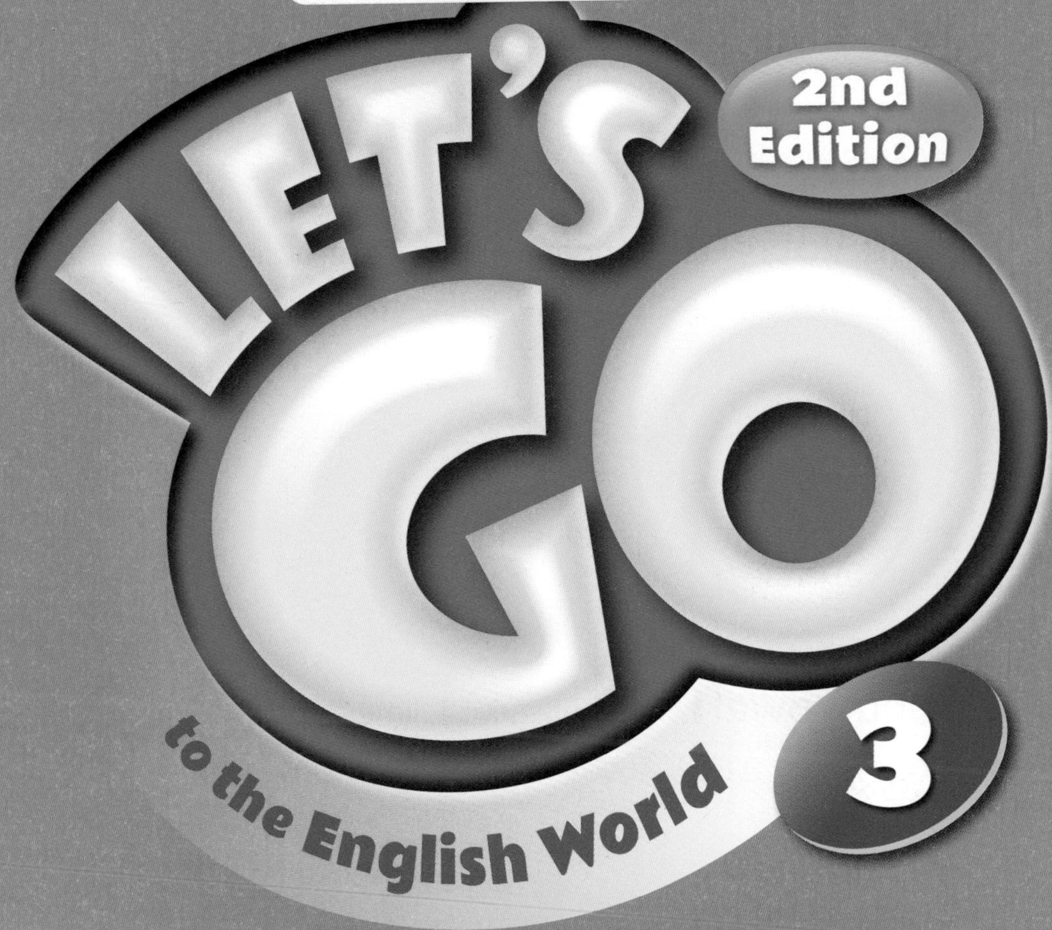
LET'S GO
2nd Edition
to the English World
3

Phonics

CHUNJAE EDUCATION, INC.

Long Vowels

CONTENTS

Magic e

- **Listen and repeat.** 01

	short		long	
	can	e	cane	
	tap	e	tape	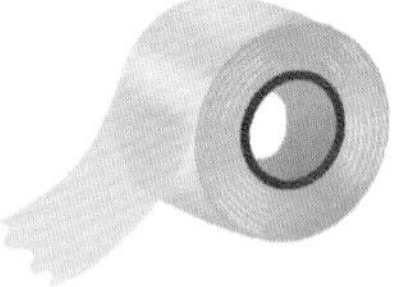
	pin	e	pine	
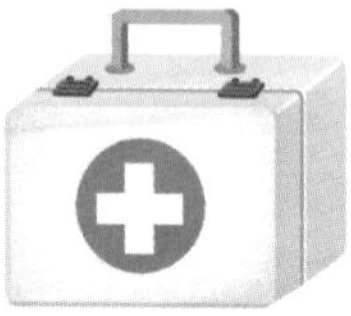	kit	e	kite	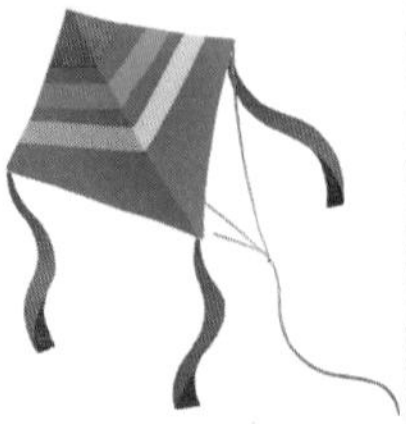

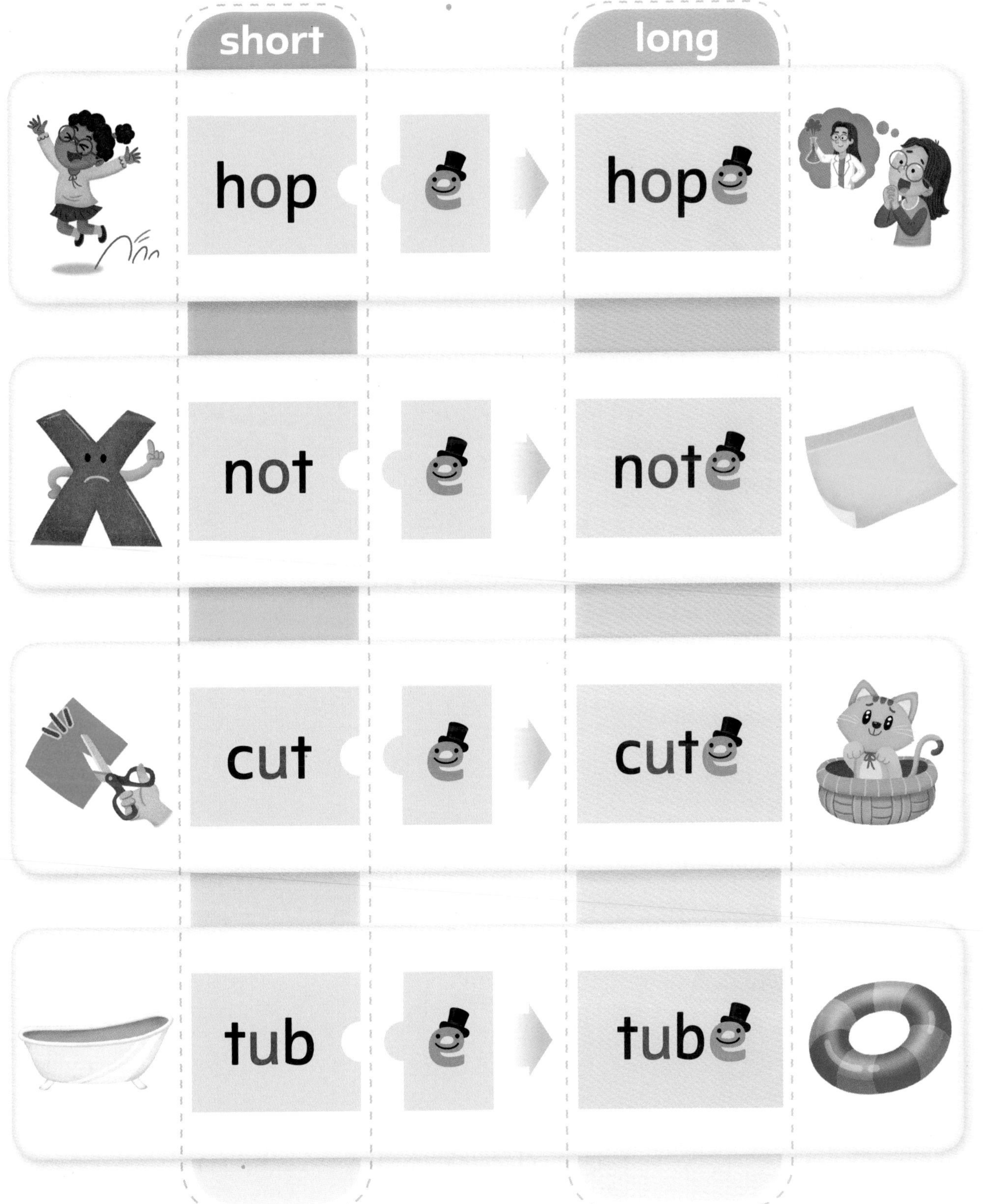
short
long
hop
hope
not
note
cut
cute
tub
tube

Unit 01

Long Vowel a

Listen and repeat. 02

a m e

g a m e

a n e

c a n e

a s e

b a s e

A Read step by step.

1. 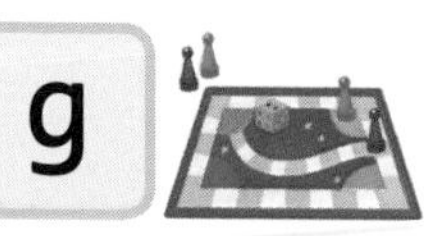
g

a m e

g a m e

2. c 

a n e

c a n e

3. 
b

a s e

b a s e

B Read and say. 03

ame
game

name

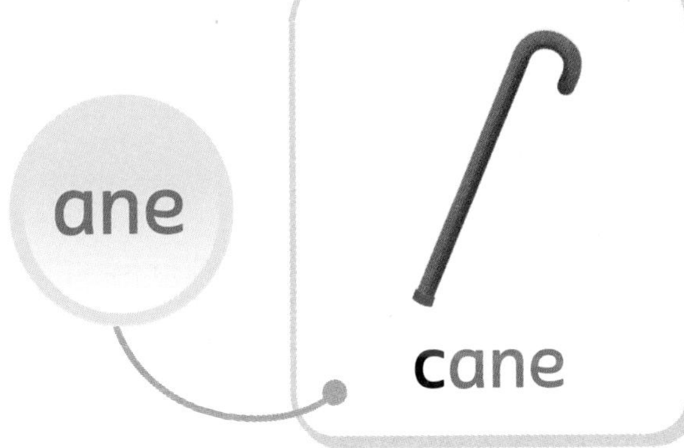
ane
cane

Jane
Jane

mane

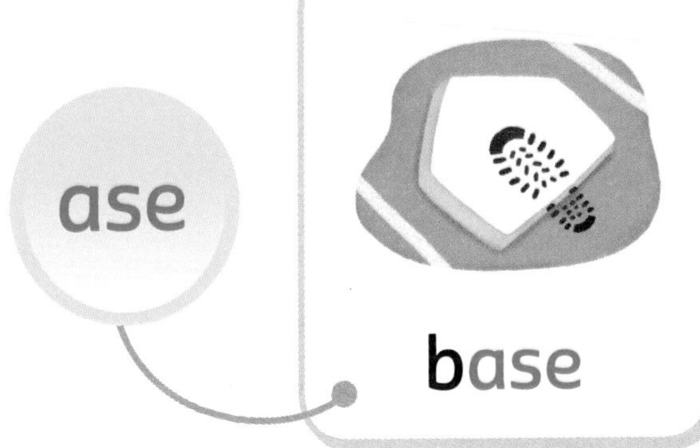
ase
base

case

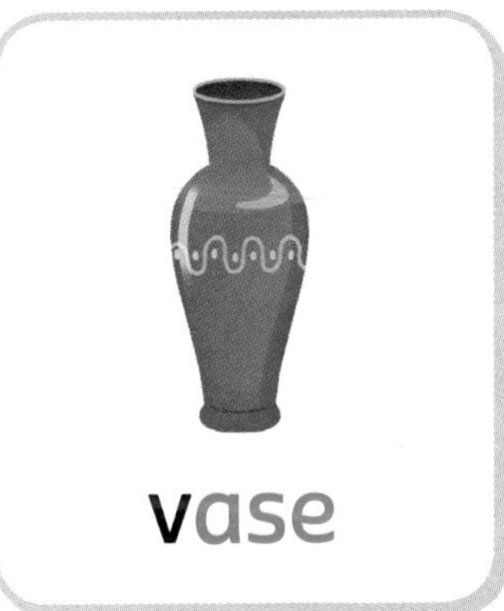
vase

C Point and chant. 04

ame
ane
ase

A Listen and stick. 05

1. 
c
ane

2. 
v
sticker

3. 
g
sticker

4. 
J
sticker

5. 
m
sticker

6. 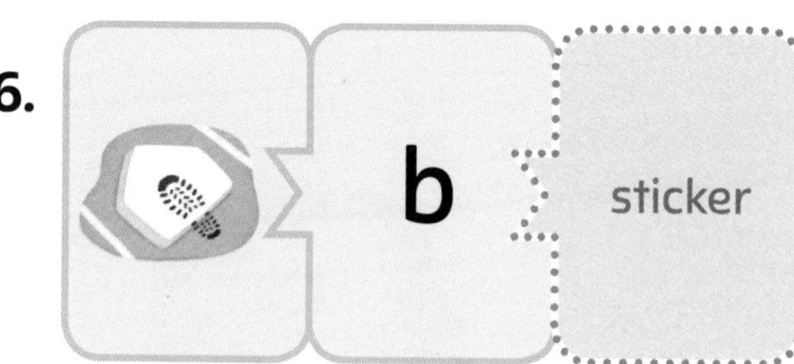
b
sticker

7. 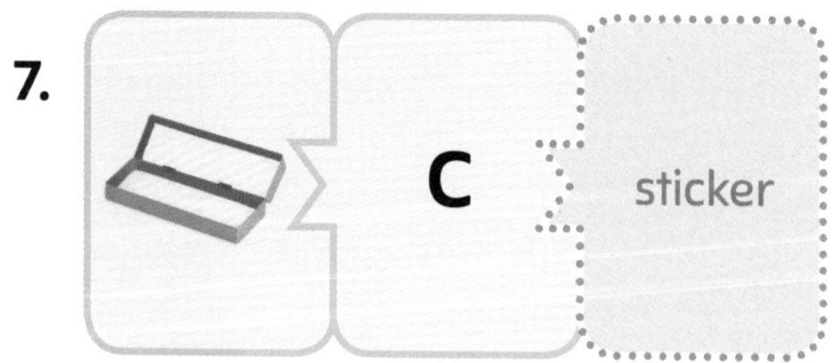
c
sticker

8. 
n
sticker

Say aloud. 1 2 3

B Match and write.

1. mane — ane | ase — base

2. c | ane | ase | J

3. g | ame | ase | v

4. n | ane | ame | c

A Listen, circle and check. 06

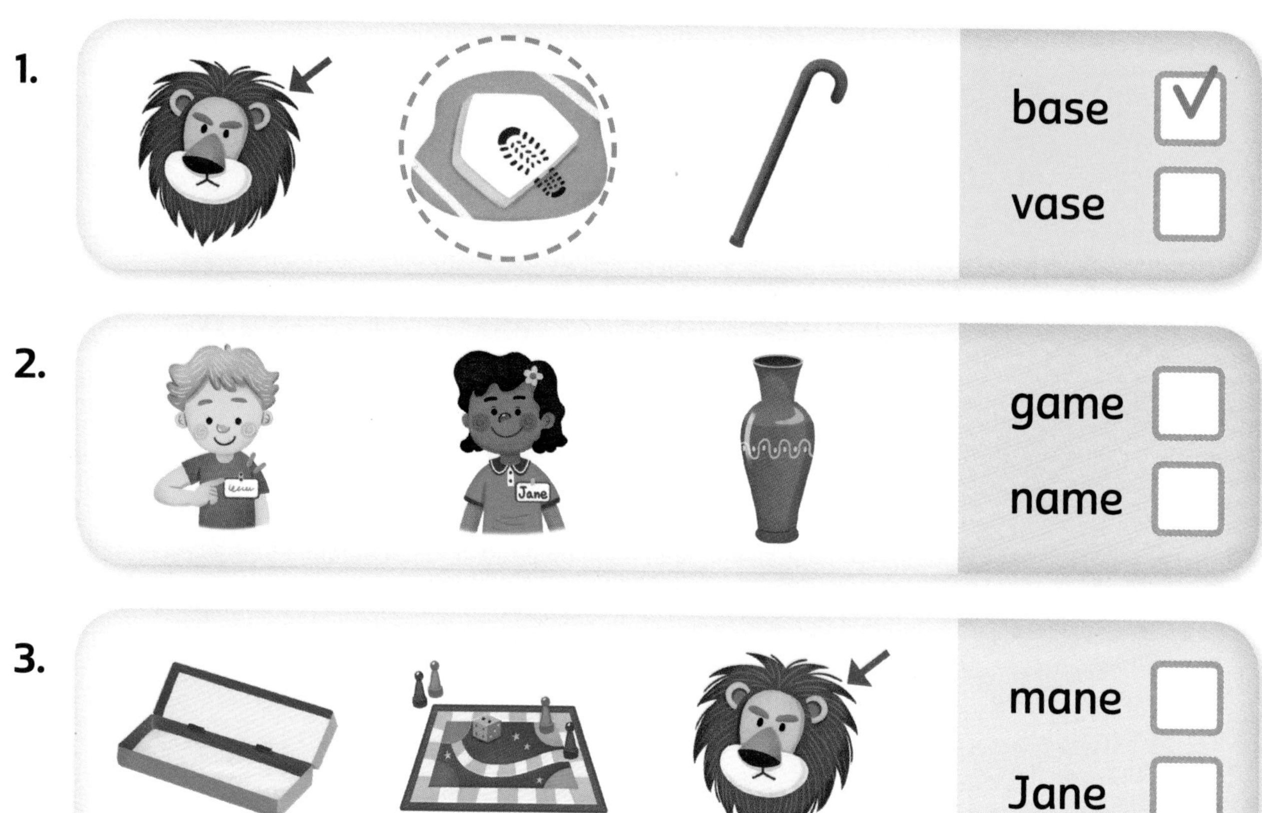
1.
base ☑
vase ☐
2.
Jane
game ☐
name ☐
3.
mane ☐
Jane ☐

B Listen and circle. 07

1. My (name / game) is on the cane.

2. A lion with a (Jane / mane) is on the base.

3. A (cane / vase) is in the case.

C Read and find.

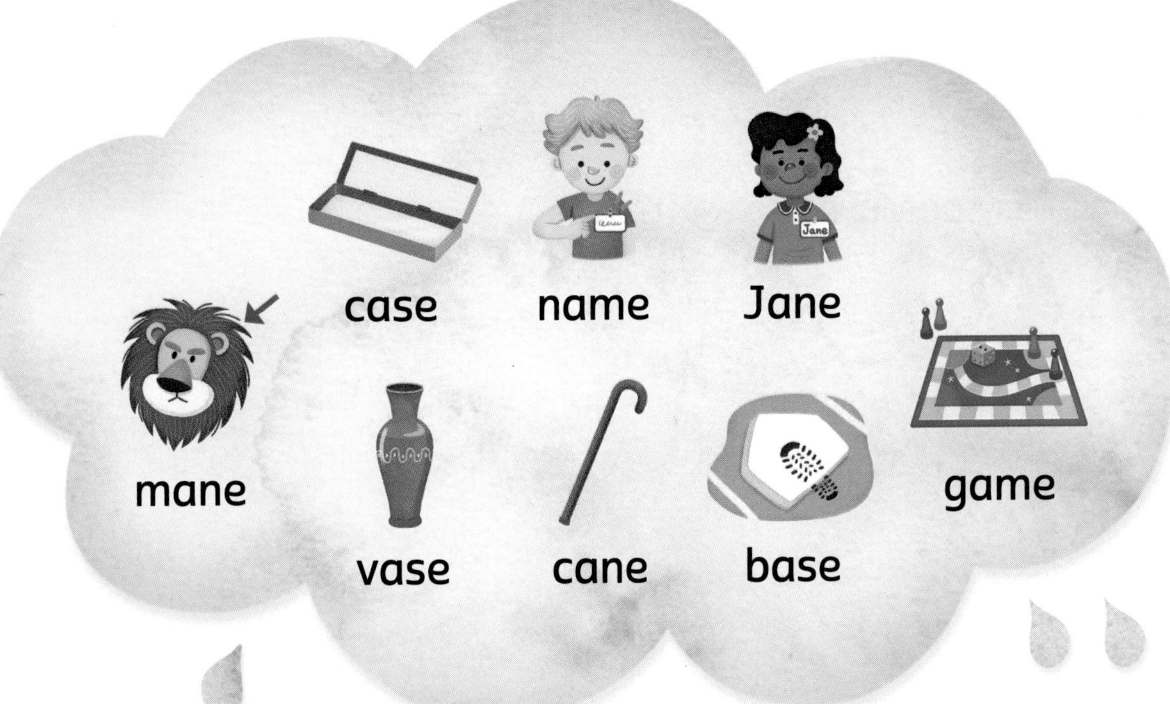
case
name
Jane
mane
vase
cane
base
game

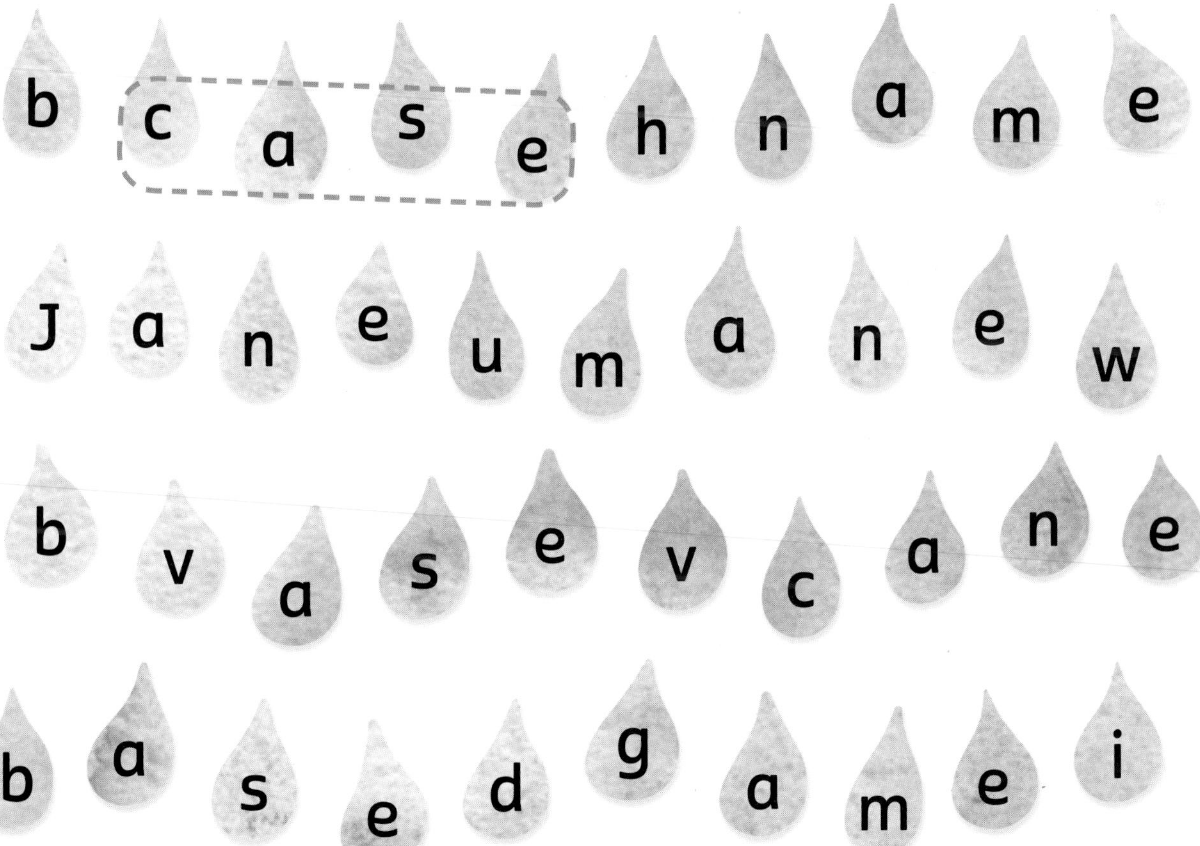
b c a s e h n a m e
J a n e u m a n e w
b v a s e v c a n e
b a s e d g a m e i

Story Time

Let's read together. 08

The cane sees a case.
The cane sees a mane, too.

Can you open it?

Hi, my name is Jane.

Hi, Jane.

Sight Words

sees can open my

Writing Time

Write and say.

1. ame ➡ game

2.  ame ➡ name

3.  ane 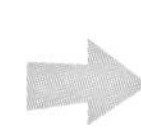 cane

4.  ane  Jane

5.  ane  mane

6. 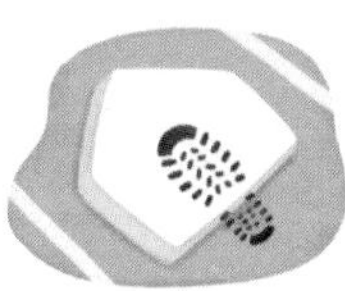 ase  base

7.  ase  case

8.  ase  vase

➡ Go to the workbook p. 2

Unit
02

Long Vowel a

- **Listen and repeat.** 09

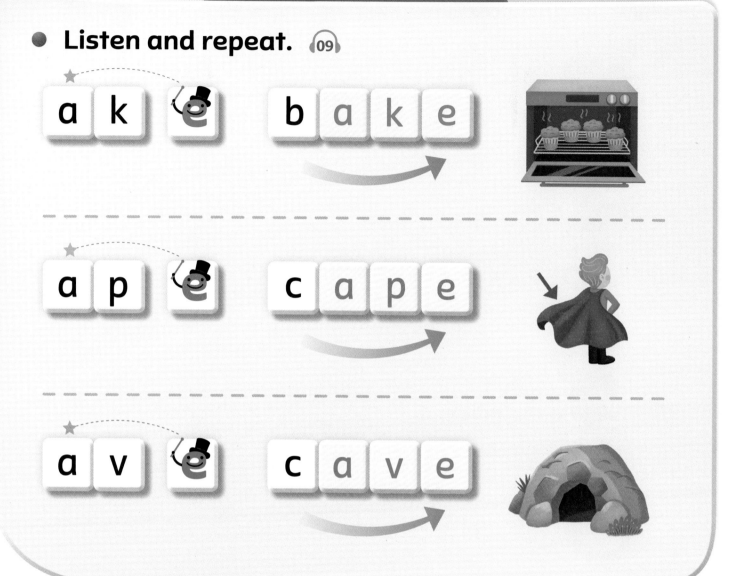

a k e → b a k e

a p e → c a p e

a v e → c a v e

A Read step by step.

1. b 
a k e
b a k e

2. c 
a p e
c a p e

3. c 
a v e
c a v e

B Read and say. 10

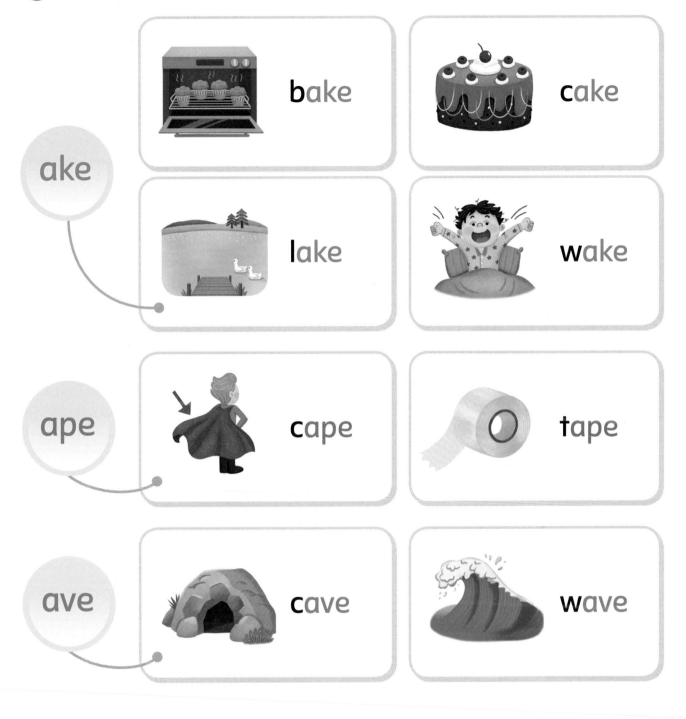

ake

bake

cake

lake

wake

ape

cape

tape

ave

cave

wave

C Point and chant. 11

ake
ape
ave

A Listen and check. (12)

1. c — ave ☑ / ake ☐
2. b — ape ☐ / ake ☐
3. t — ake ☐ / ape ☐
4. w — ake ☐ / ave ☐
5. c — ave ☐ / ape ☐
6. c — ape ☐ / ake ☐

7. w — ave ☐ / ape ☐
8. l — ake ☐ / ave ☐

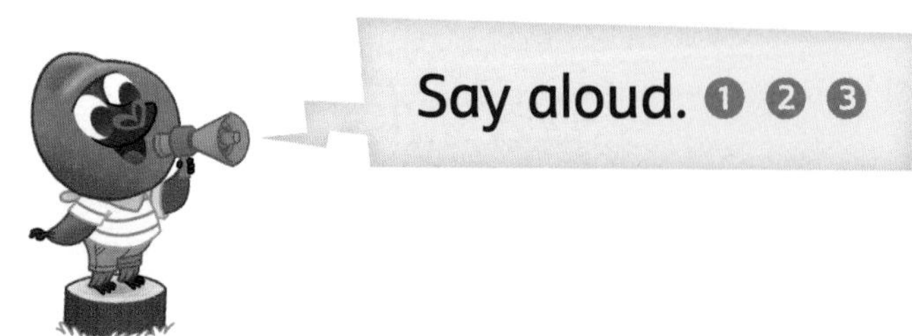
Say aloud. ❶ ❷ ❸

B Match and write.

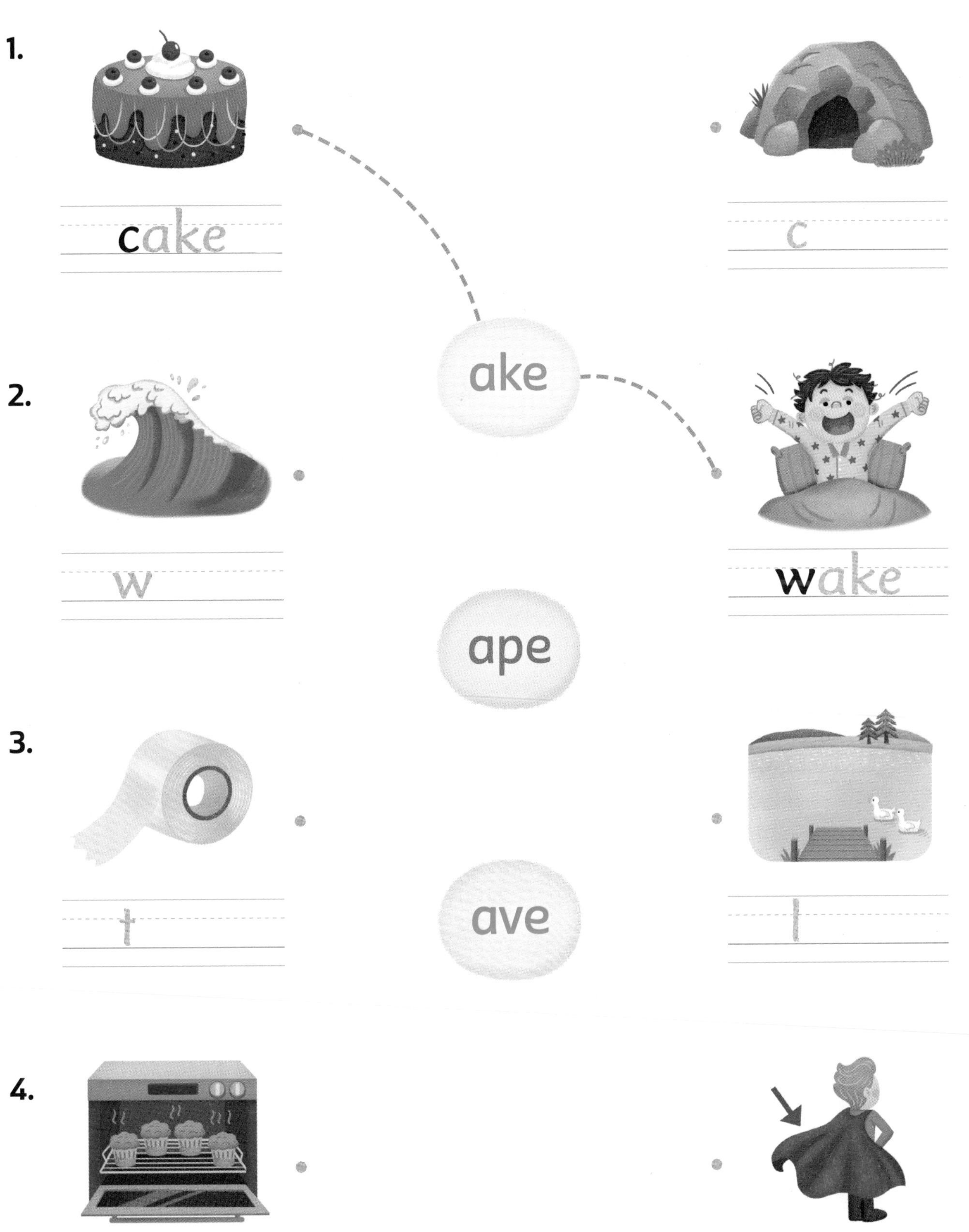
1.
cake
c
ake
2.
w
wake
ape
3.
t
l
ave
4.
b
c

A Listen, circle and color. 13

1. c a k e l p

2. w a p e c v

3. c a k e t p

4. b a k e w v

B Listen and circle. 14

1. We (bake / wake) a cake.

2. I see a (wave / cave) by the lake.

3. Ben has a (cake / cape) and tape.

C Read and find.

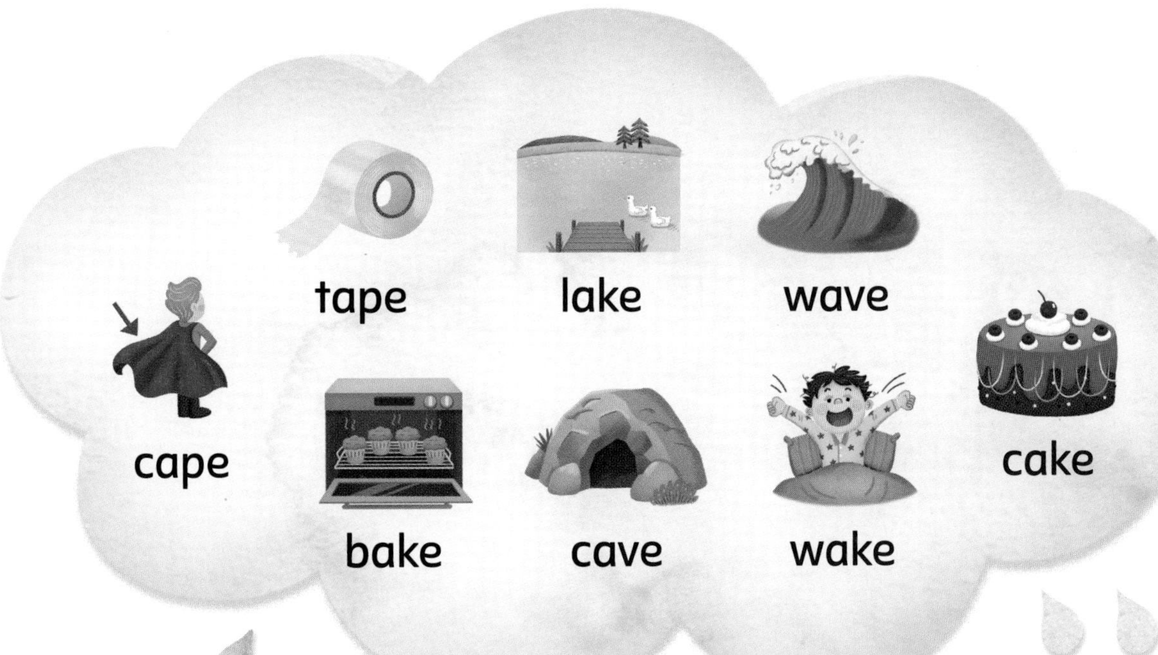
tape
lake
wave
cape
bake
cave
wake
cake

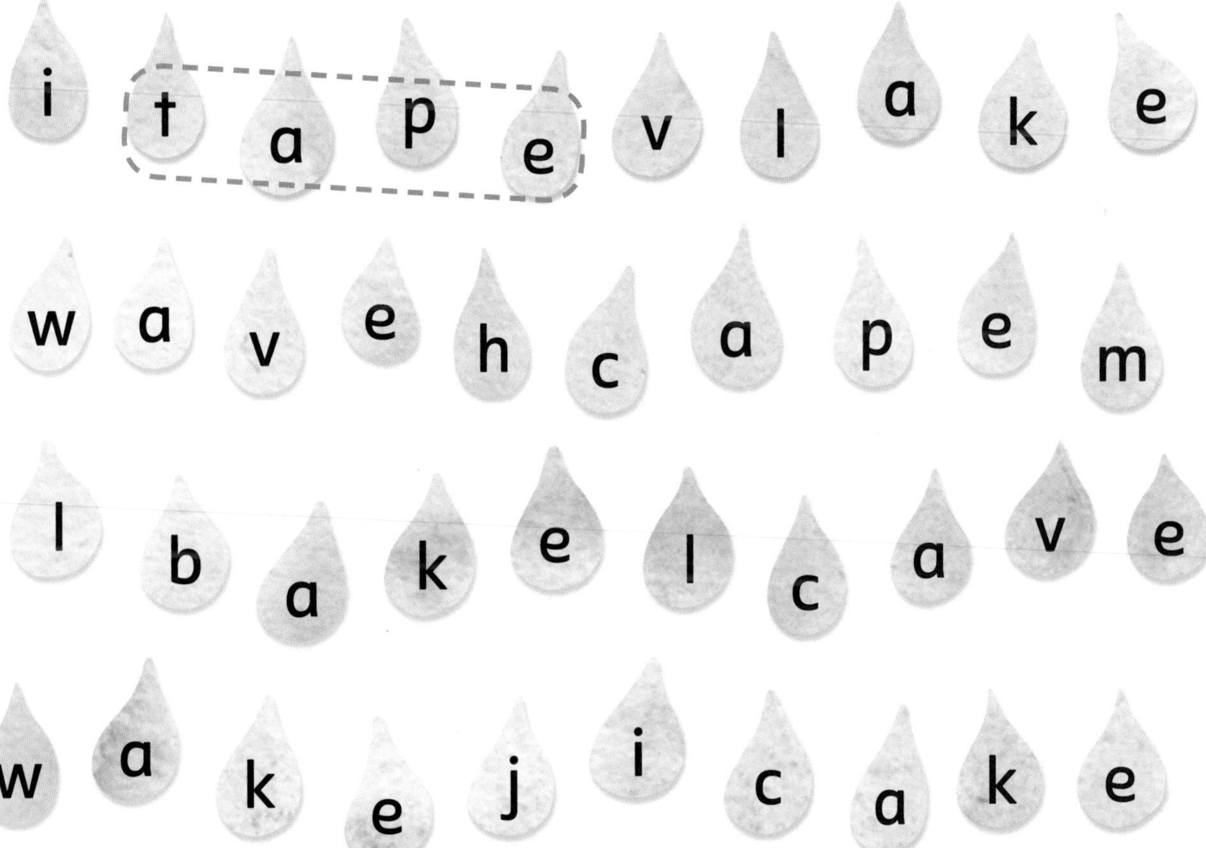
i t a p e v l a k e
w a v e h c a p e m
l b a k e l c a v e
w a k e j i c a k e

Story Time

Let's read together. 15

T H D A

The tape wears a cape.
The tape sees a cake.

I can help you.

A boat is on the lake.
The tape sees the wave.

Thank you!

Sight Words

help is on thank

Write and say.

1.  ake ➡ bake

2.  ake ➡ cake

3.  ake  lake

4.  ake  wake

5.  ape  cape

6.  ape  tape

7.  ave  cave

8.  ave  wave

➡ Go to the workbook p. 6

Unit 03

Long Vowel i

● **Listen and repeat.** 16

i k e

b i k e

i m e

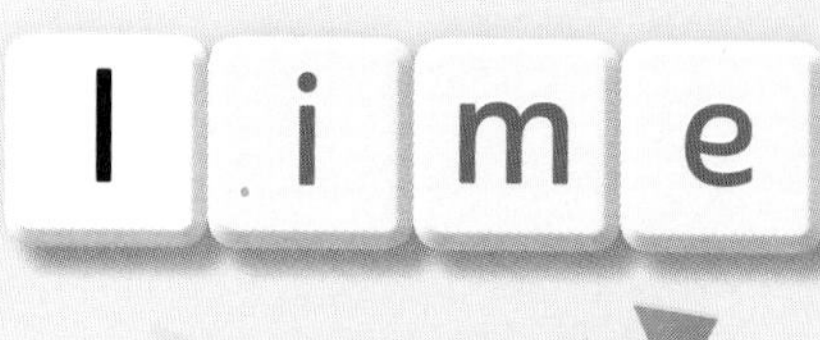

l i m e

i n e

p i n e

A Read step by step.

1. b

i k e

b i k e

2. l

i m e

l i m e

3. p

i n e

p i n e

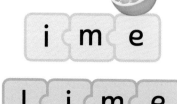

B Read and say. 17

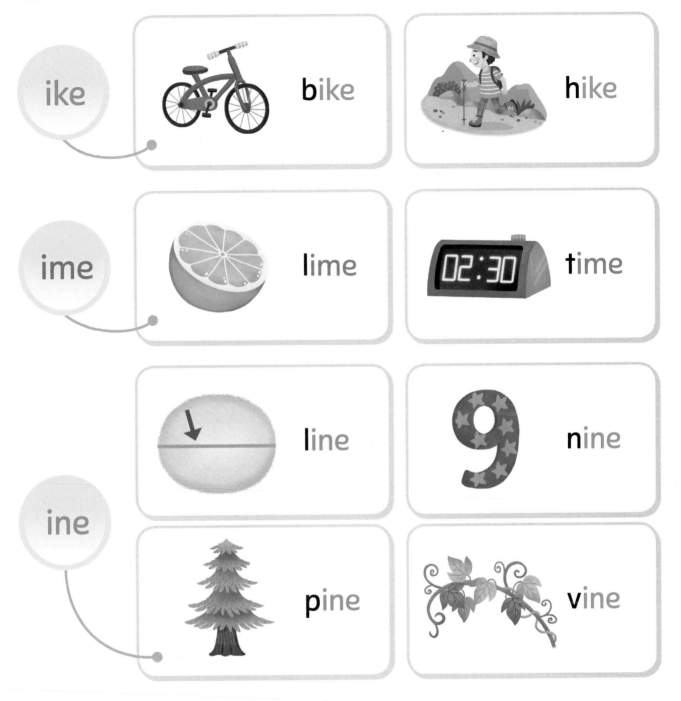

ike

bike | hike

ime

lime | time

ine

line | nine

pine | vine

C Point and chant. 18

ike
ime
ine

A Listen and stick. 19

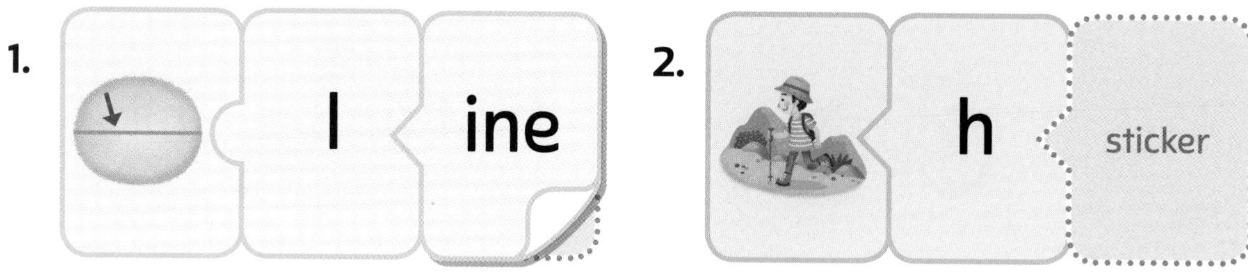
1.
l
ine
2.
h
sticker

3.
02:30
t
sticker
4.
v
sticker

5.
b
sticker
6.
p
sticker

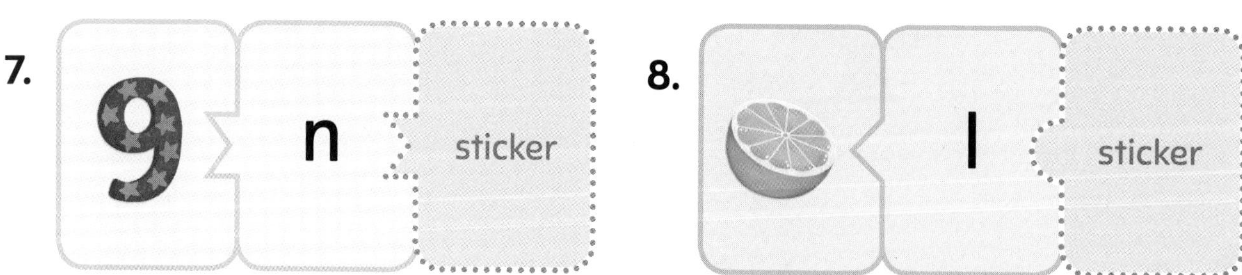
7.
9
n
sticker
8.
l
sticker

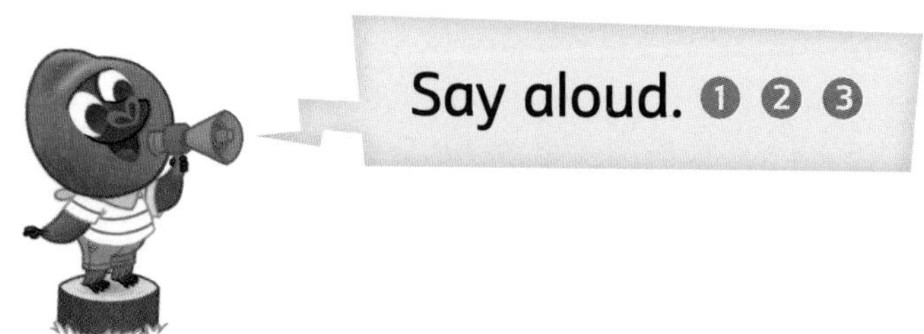
Say aloud. ❶ ❷ ❸

B Match and write.

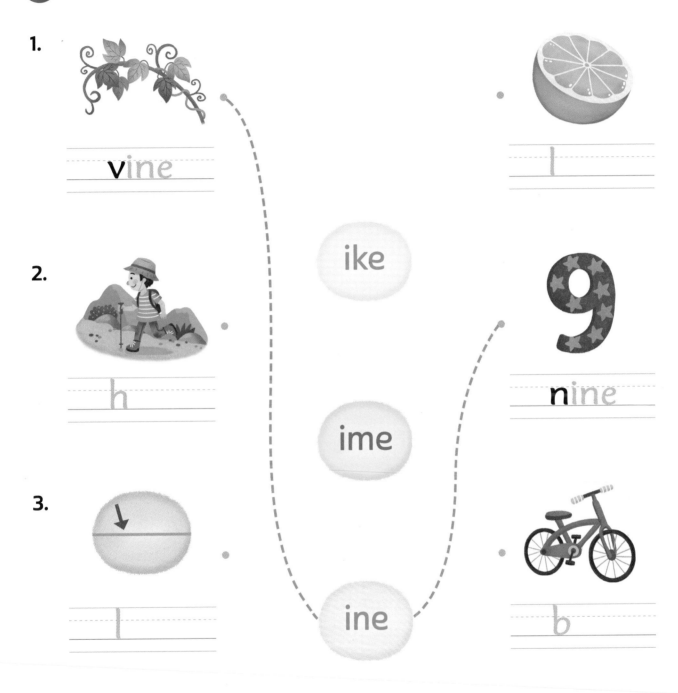

1. vine

l

ike

2. h

nine

ime

3. l

b

ine

4. 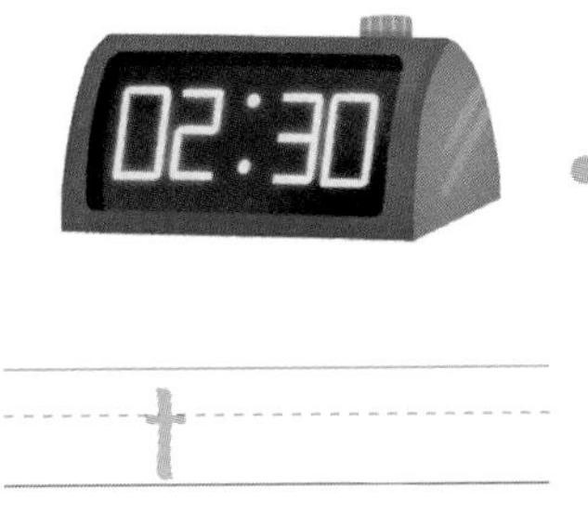

t

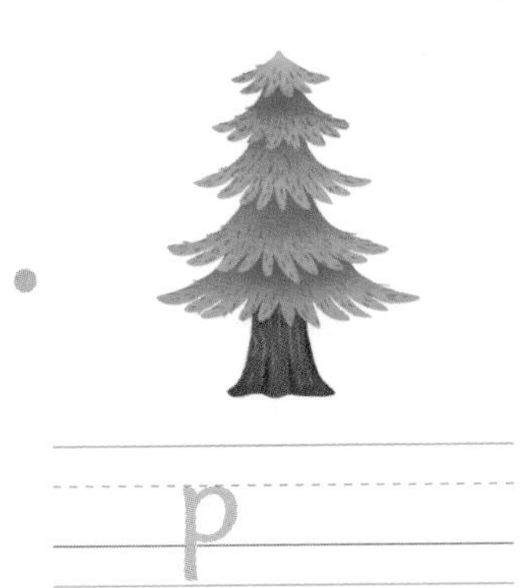

p

Listen, circle and check. (20)

1.

02:30

vine ☐
pine ☐

2.

9

bike ☐
hike ☐

3.

lime ☐
time ☐

B Listen and circle. (21)

1. 

They hike up to the (pine / nine).

2. 
9

A nine is on the (hike / bike).

3. 

There is a (lime / time) on the line.

C Read and find.

02:30

time

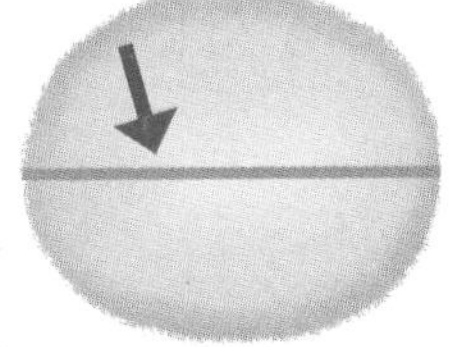

line

vine

hike

t	v	w	p	i	n	e	c
b	i	j	h	e	b	l	m
p	n	m	a	i	i	i	r
l	e	v	e	i	k	n	f
t	i	b	i	y	e	e	o
k	v	m	t	e	w	t	i
n	i	n	e	j	o	d	s

bike

nine

lime

pine

Story Time

Let's read together. 22

Can you see the limes?

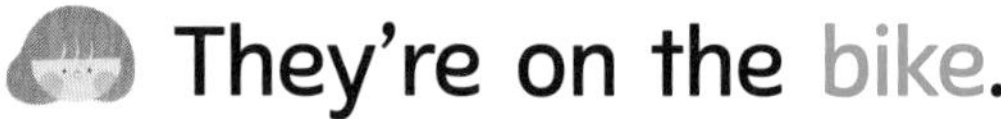
They're on the bike.

Can you see a nine?

It's on the vine.

No, it's not a nine.
It's a six.

Oh, it's on the pine!

Sight Words

you they're no not

Writing Time

STEP 4

Write and say.

1.  ike 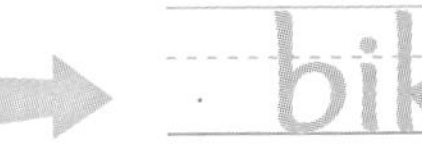 bike

2.  ike  hike

3.  ime  lime

4.  ime  time

5. 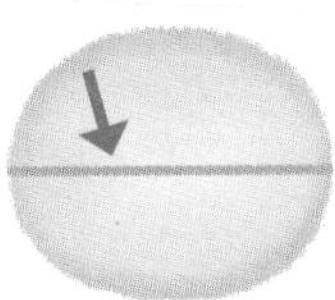 ine  line

6.  ine 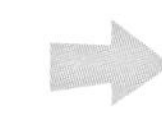 nine

7.  ine  pine

8.  ine  vine

➡ Go to the workbook p. 10

Unit
04

Long Vowel i

- **Listen and repeat.** 23

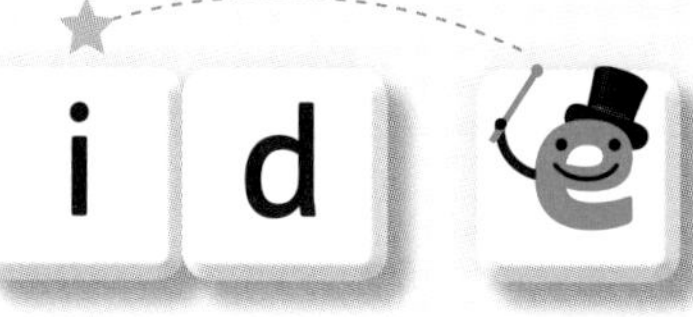
i d e

h i d e

i t e

b i t e

i v e
d i v e

A Read step by step.

1. h

i d e
h i d e

2. b

i t e
b i t e

3. d

i v e
d i v e

B Read and say. 24

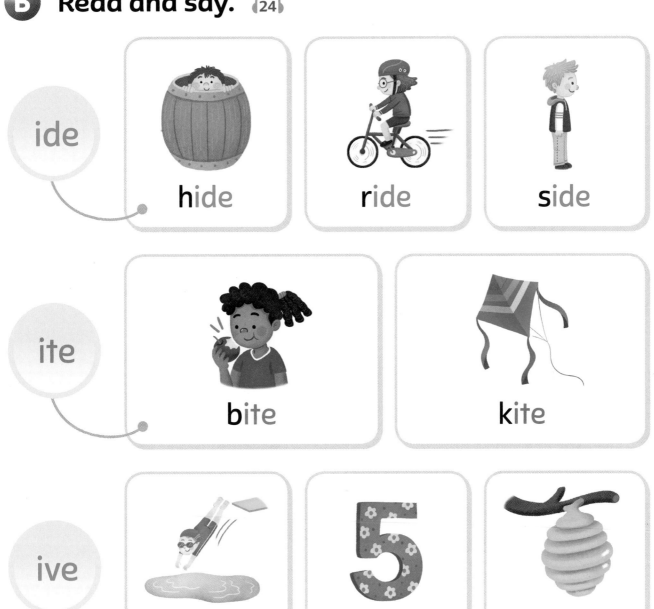

ide

hide | ride | side

ite

bite | kite

ive

dive | five | hive

C Point and chant. 25

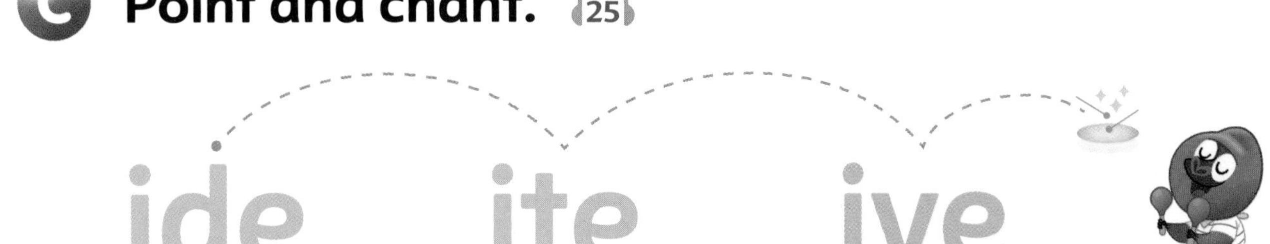
ide
ite
ive

A Listen and check. 26

1. d
- ide ☐
- ive ☑

2. b
- ite ☐
- ide ☐

3. h
- ite ☐
- ide ☐

4. f
- ive ☐
- ide ☐

5. s
- ide ☐
- ite ☐

6. k
- ive ☐
- ite ☐

7. h
- ive ☐
- ite ☐

8. r
- ide ☐
- ive ☐

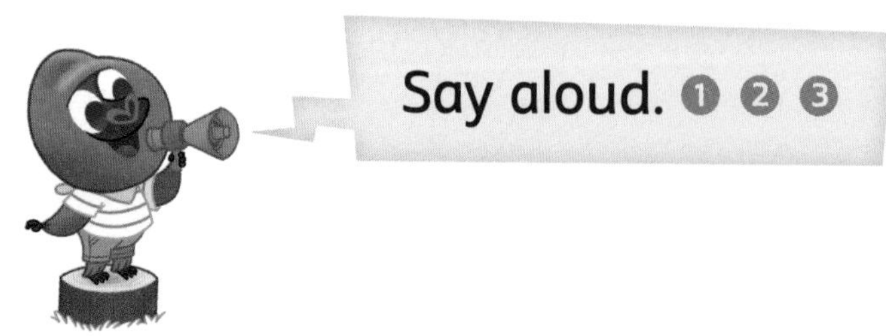
Say aloud. ❶ ❷ ❸

B Match and write.

1. ive / ide

hive — side

2. ide / ive

r — f

3. ide / ite

b — h

4. ite / ive

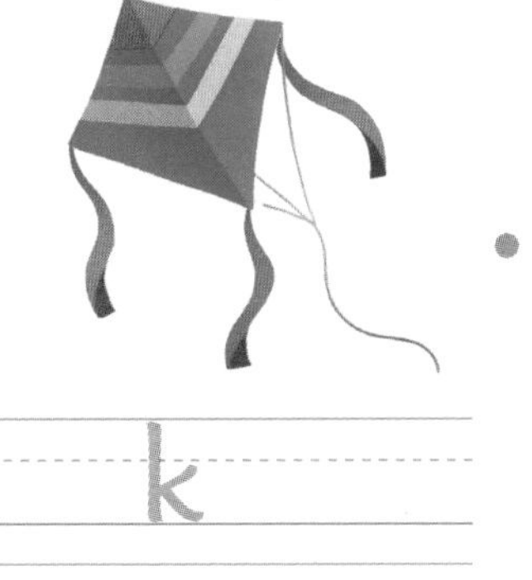

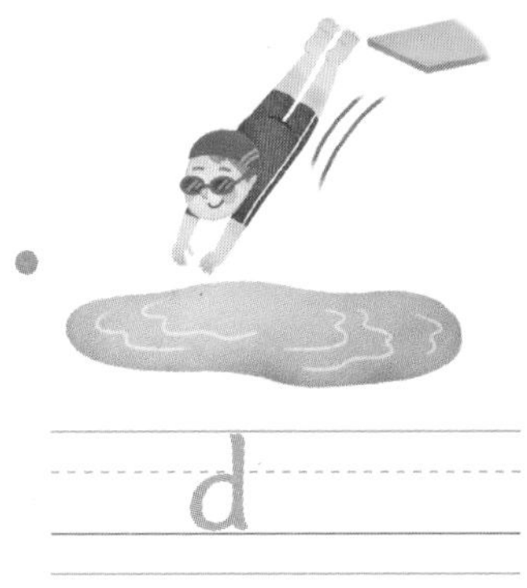

k — d

A Listen, circle and color. 27

1.

f
v
i
e
r
d

2.

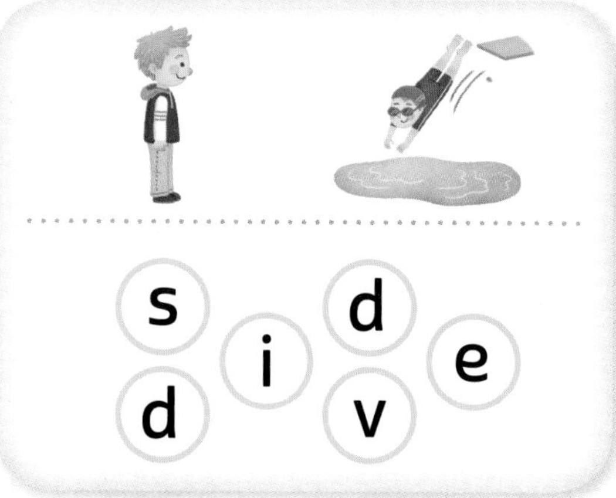
s
d
i
e
d
v

3.

b
v
i
e
h
t

4.

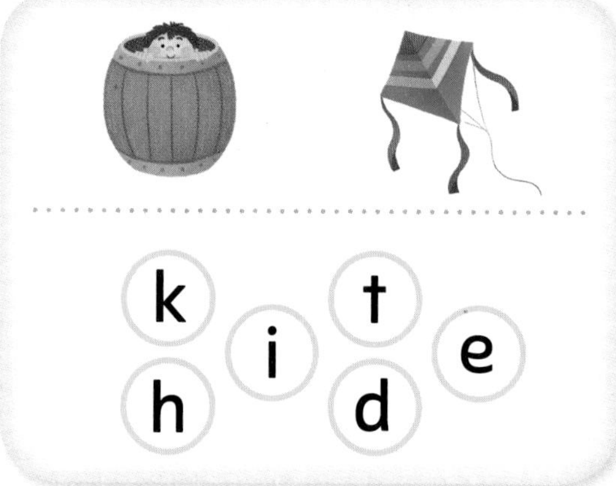
k
t
i
e
h
d

B Listen and circle. 28

1. 

The cat likes to bite a (hive / kite).

2. 

A bee can (hide / five) in a hive.

3. 

Five ants (ride / dive) into the water.

C Read and find.

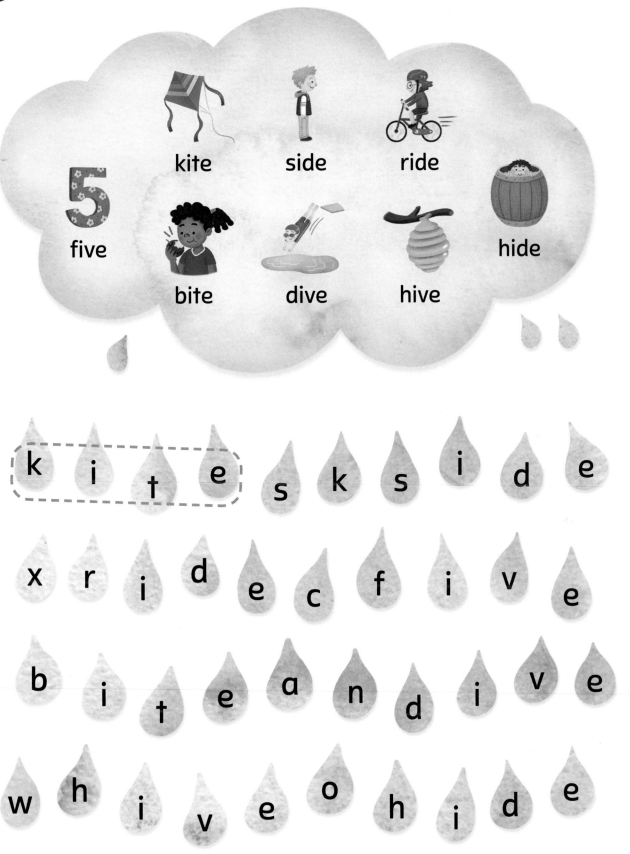

five kite side ride hide bite dive hive

k i t e s k s i d e

x r i d e c f i v e

b i t e a n d i v e

w h i v e o h i d e

Story Time

Let's read together. (29)

Ted has five dogs.
They like to hide the kite.
They like to bite the kite.

Ted finds a hive.
He puts the hive in the house.

The dogs dive into the water.

Sight Words

has finds puts water

Writing Time

Write and say.

1.  ide → hide

2.  ide → ride

3.  ide  side

4.  ite  bite

5.  ite  kite

6.  ive  dive

7.  ive  five

8.  ive  hive

➡ Go to the workbook p. 14

Unit 05

Long Vowel O

Listen and repeat. 30

o p e
h o p e

o s e
h o s e

A Read step by step.

1.
h
o p e
h o p e
2.
h
o s e
h o s e

B Read and say. 31

ope
hope

pope

rope

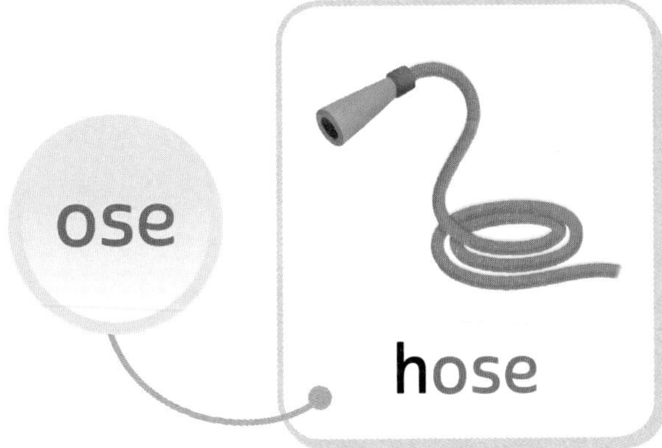
ose
hose

nose

rose

C Point and chant. 32

ope ose

A Listen and stick. 33

1.
h
ose
2.
p
sticker

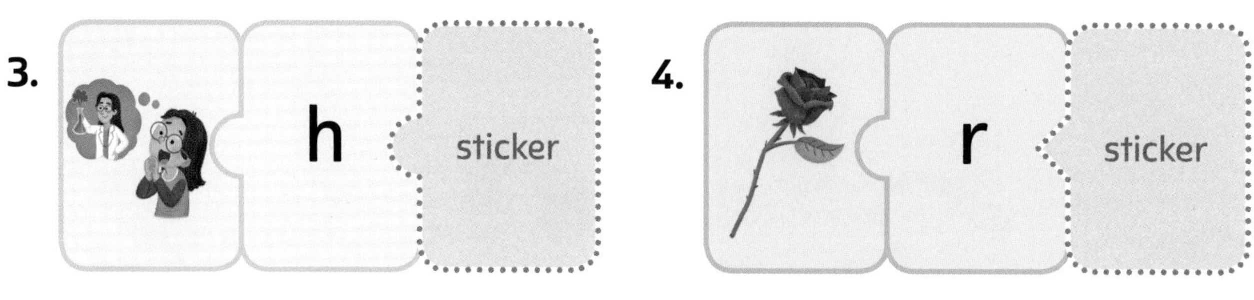

3.
h
sticker
4.
r
sticker

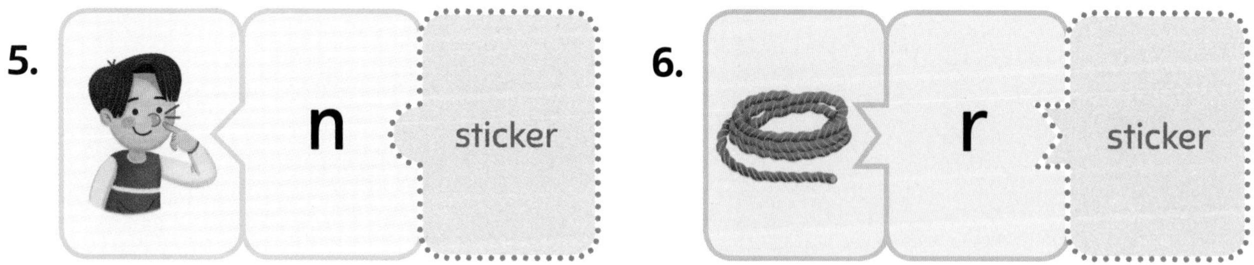

5.
n
sticker
6.
r
sticker

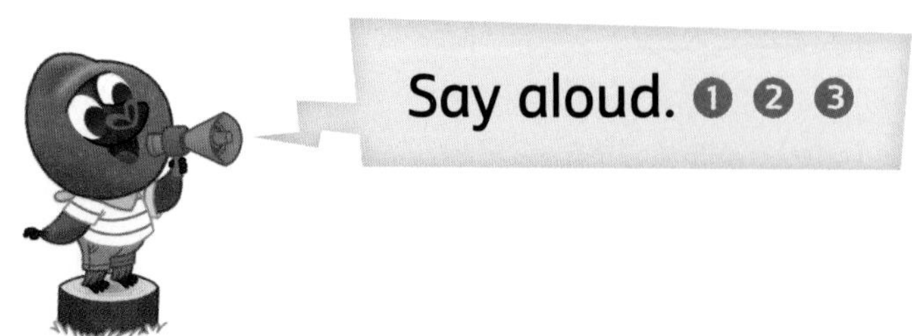

Say aloud. 1 2 3

B Match and write.

1. 

rose

2. 

p

3. 

h

ope

ose

4. 

h

5. 

n

6. 

r

Listen, circle and check. 34

1.

nose ☐
rose ☐

2.

rope ☐
pope ☐

3.

hose ☐
nose ☐

B Listen and circle. 35

1. 

The dog's nose smells a (hose / rose).

2. 

She has a rope and a (hose / hope).

3. 

I hope to meet the (pope / nose).

C Read and find.

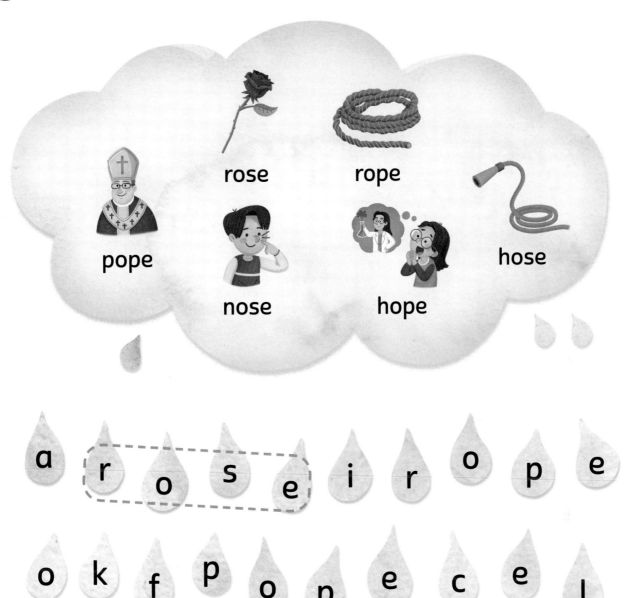

pope

rose

nose

rope

hope

hose

a r o s e i r o p e

o k f p o p e c e l

n o s e m h o p e j

g b w q h o s e d k

Story Time

Let's read together. 36

"Oh, it's very hot."

The rose sees a hose.
"I can use a rope."

Water comes out from the hose.
The rose gets wet.

"Oh, no!
It's an elephant's nose!"

Sight Words

very hot comes gets

Write and say.

1.
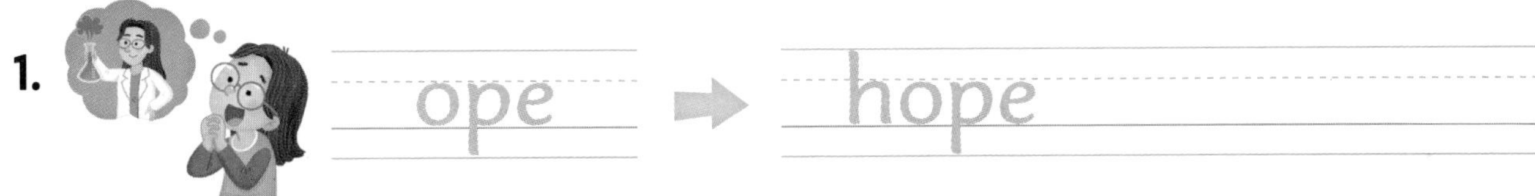
ope
hope

2.
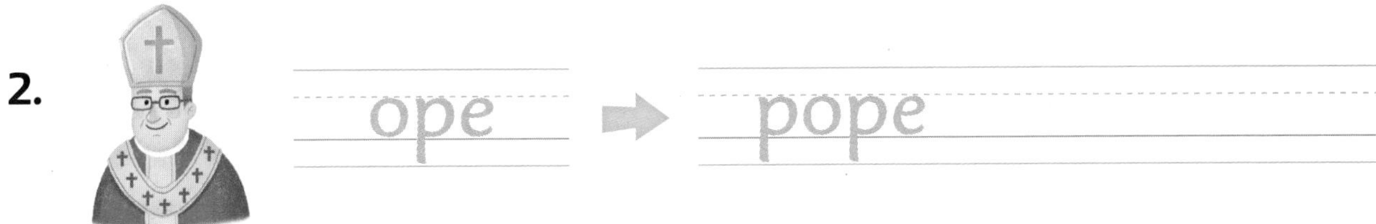
ope
pope

3.
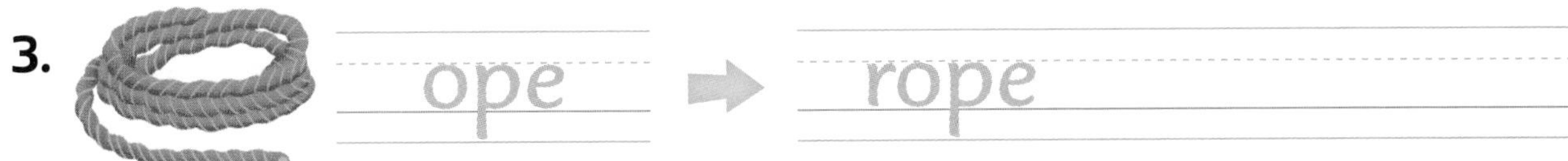
ope
rope

4.
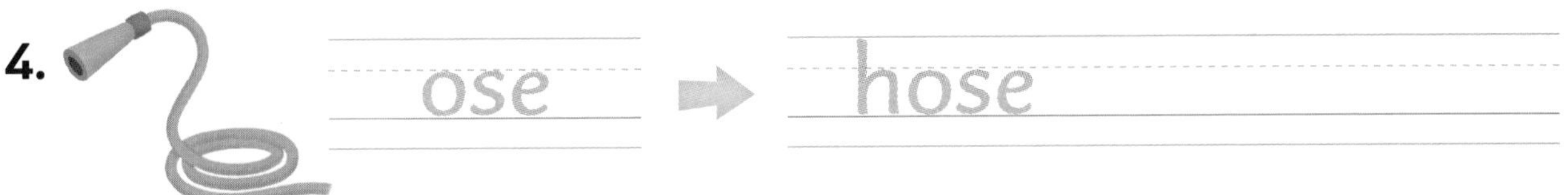
ose
hose

5.
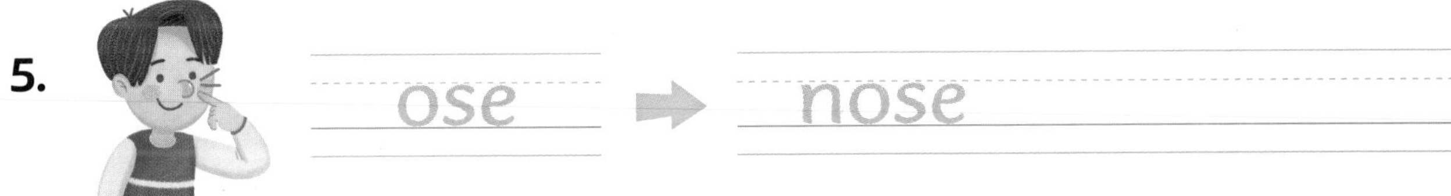
ose
nose

6.

ose
rose

➡ Go to the workbook p. 18

Review 1

A Listen and match. 37

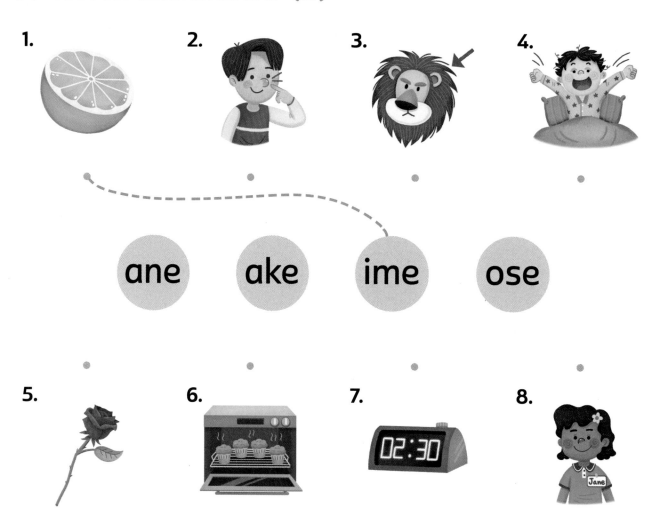

1. 2. 3. 4.

ane ake ime ose

5. 6. 7. 8.

B Look and number.

1. dive 4 2. hike 3. name 4. hope

C Read and write.

line	hive	game	hose
cave	bike	rope	~~hide~~

1. hide
2.
3.
4.
5.
6.
7.
8.

D Listen and color. 38

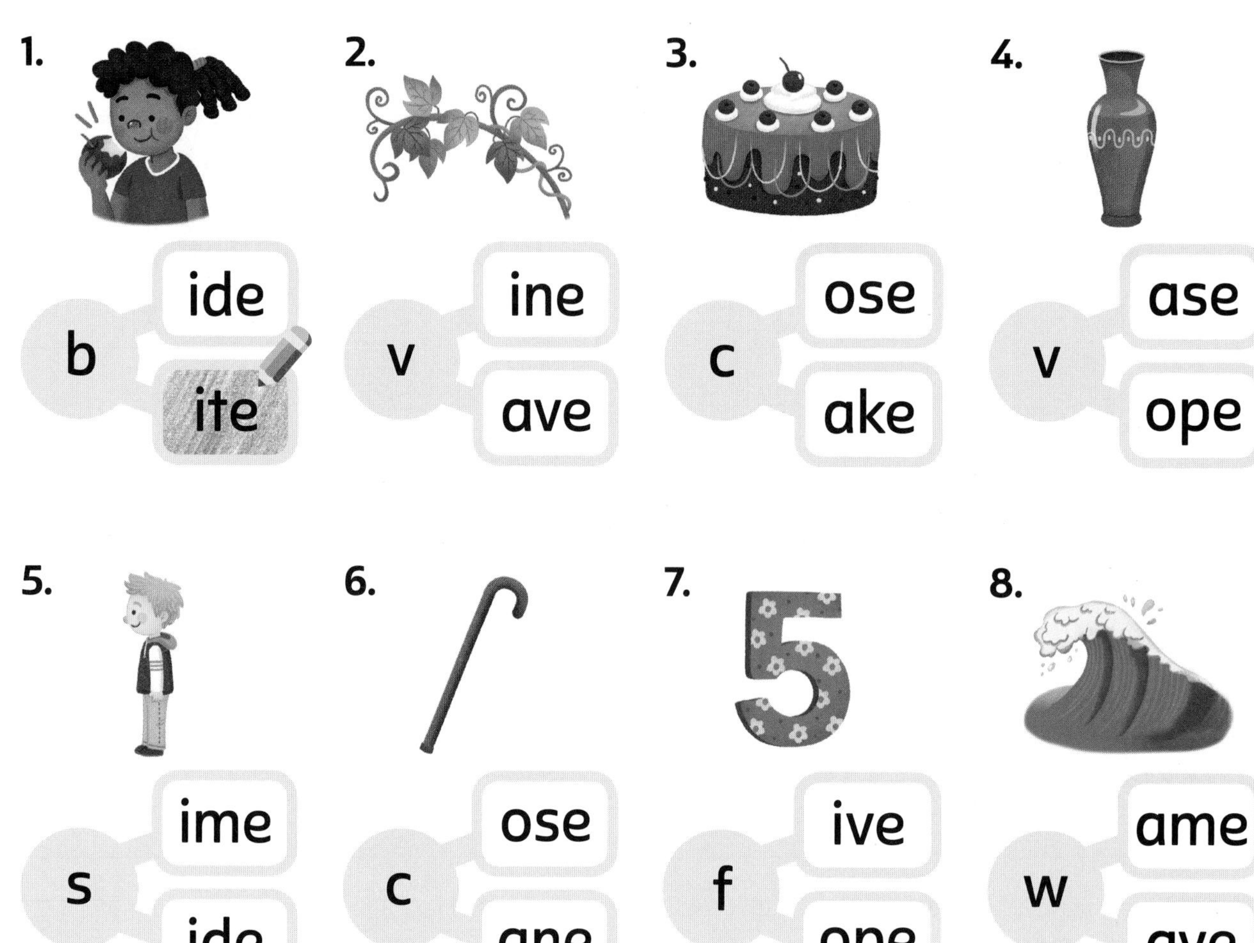
1.
b
ide
ite
2.
v
ine
ave
3.
c
ose
ake
4.
v
ase
ope
5.
s
ime
ide
6.
c
ose
ane
7.
f
ive
ope
8.
w
ame
ave

E Circle and write.

1. ave ine

nine

2. ide ope

r

3. ake ame

l

F Look and write.

kite	pope	~~base~~	rope
cape	bite	tape	case

-ase

base

-ape

-ite

-ope

➡ Go to the workbook p. 22

Unit 06

Long Vowel O

Listen and repeat. 39

h o l e

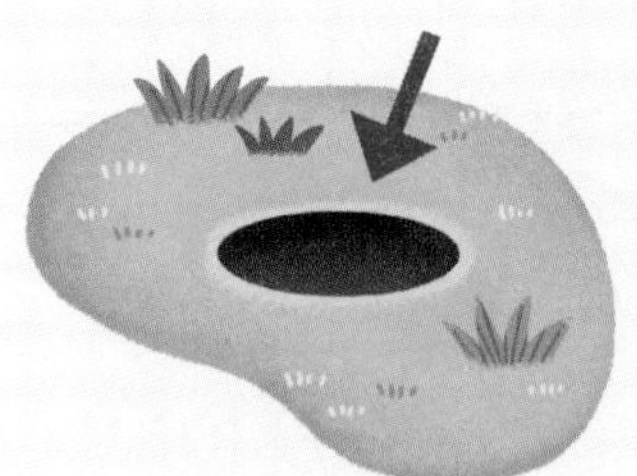

b o n e

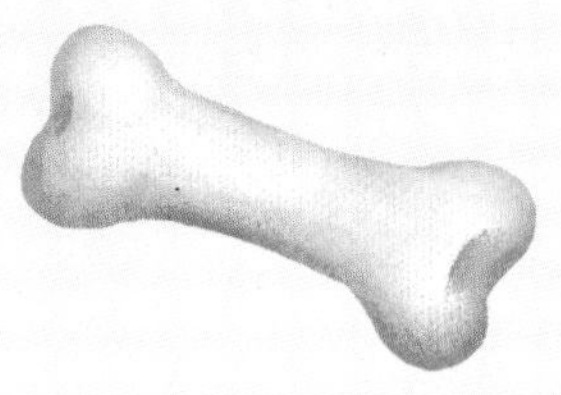

n o t e

A Read step by step.

1.

h

o l e

h o l e

2.

b

o n e

b o n e

3.

n

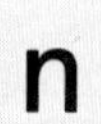

o t e

n o t e

B Read and say. 40

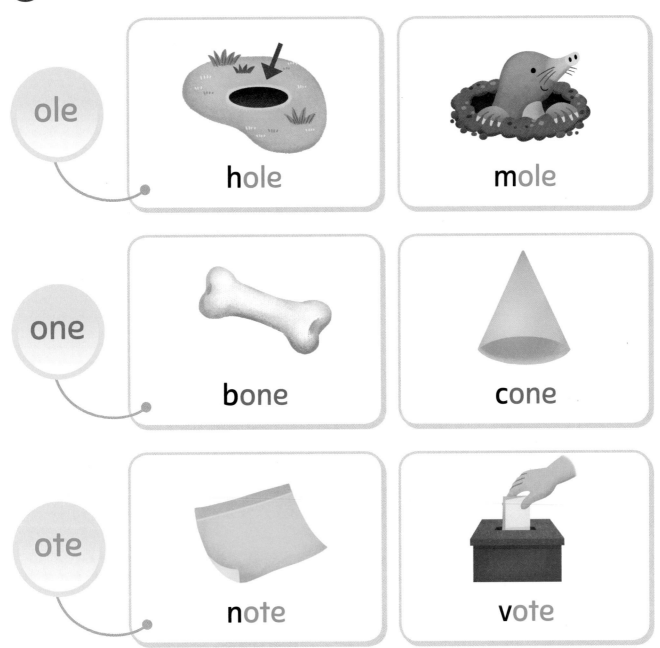

ole

hole

mole

one

bone

cone

ote

note

vote

C Point and chant. 41

ole one ote

A Listen and check. 42

1.
b
one ✓
ole
2.
m
ote
ole

3.
n
ole
ote
4.
c
one
ole

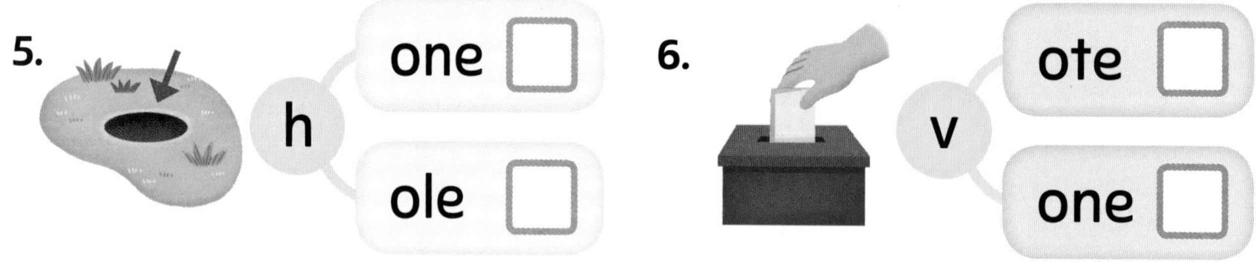
5.
h
one
ole
6.
v
ote
one

Say aloud. ❶ ❷ ❸

B Match and write.

1. 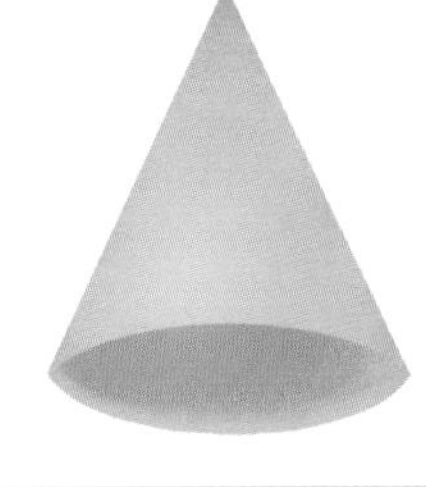

cone

2. 

v

3. 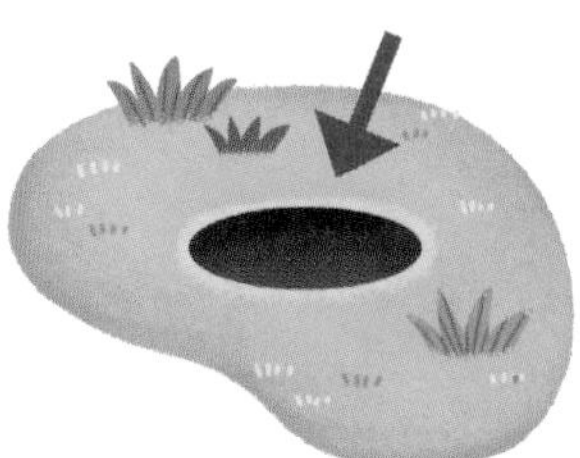

h

ole one ote

4. 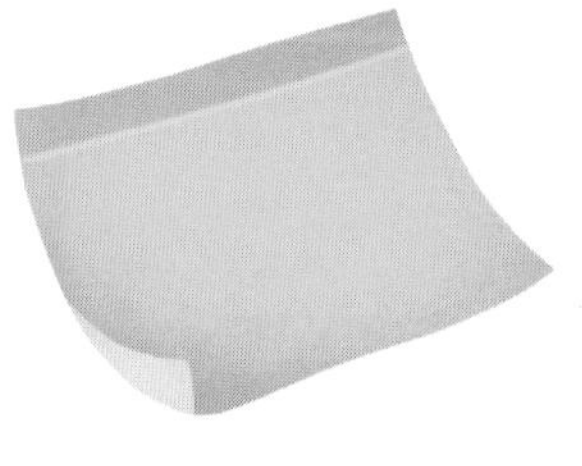

n

5. 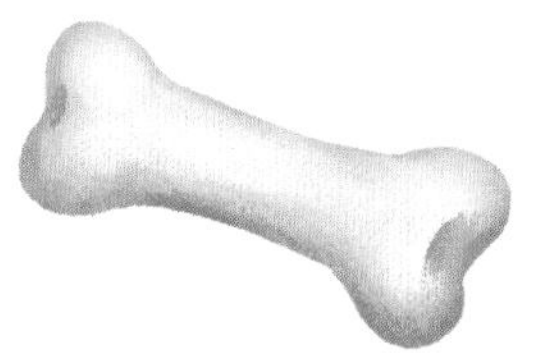

b

6. 

m

A Listen, circle and color. 43

1.

c
n
o
e
n
t

2.

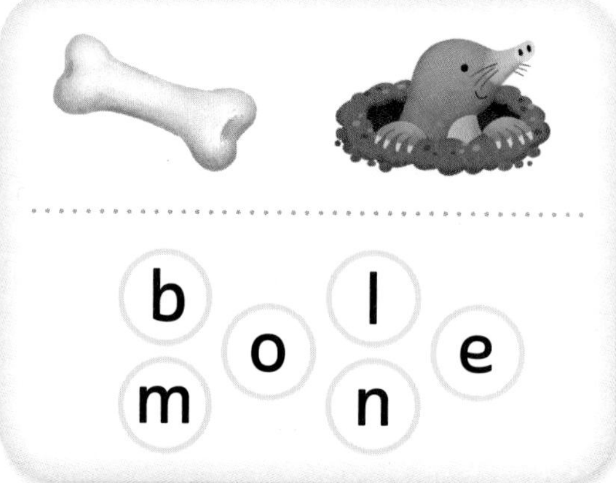

b
l
o
e
m
n

3.

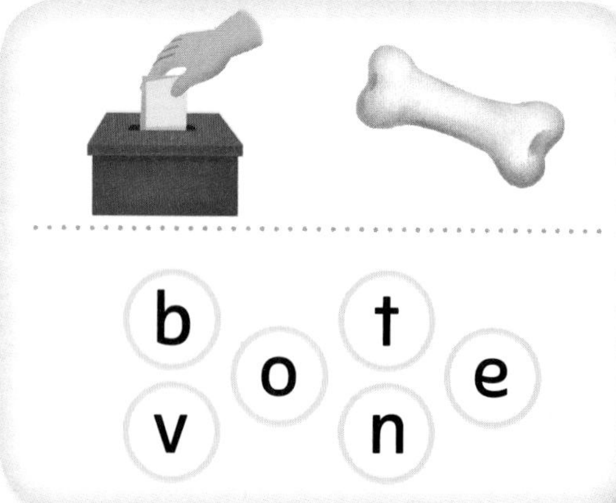

b
t
o
e
v
n

4.

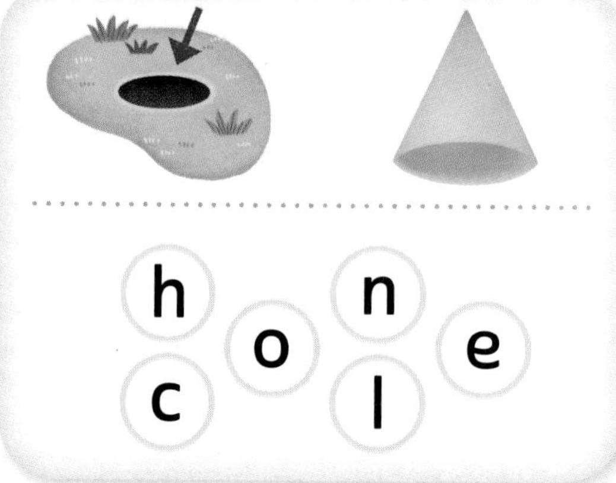

h
n
o
e
c
l

B Listen and circle. 44

1. 

A note is under the (hole / cone).

2. 

A dog sees a bone in a (mole / hole).

3. 

The mole wants to (vote / note).

C Read and find.

mole

vote

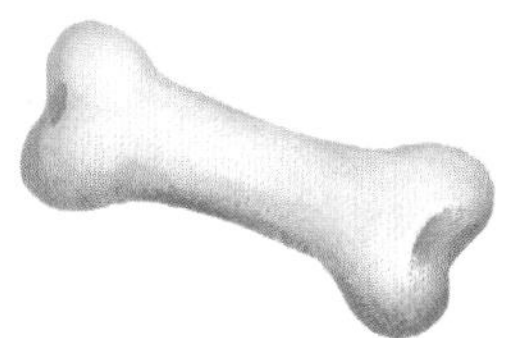

bone

m	o	l	e	a	y	s	k
u	p	v	g	z	c	k	d
h	f	g	o	i	o	r	p
b	w	c	j	t	n	h	u
o	k	n	o	t	e	f	g
n	d	r	a	q	x	m	i
e	i	j	h	o	l	e	w

note

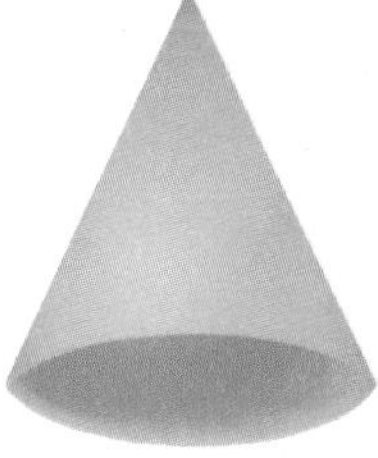

cone

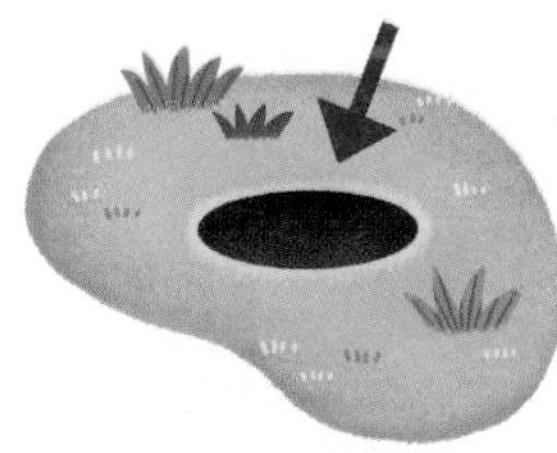

hole

Story Time

Let's read together. 45

The dog looks for a bone.
He hops over the cone.
He falls into a hole.

The dog sees a mole in the hole.
"Hi, can you help me?"

Thank you!

The mole gives the bone to the dog.

Sight Words

looks falls gives

Writing Time

Write and say.

1. 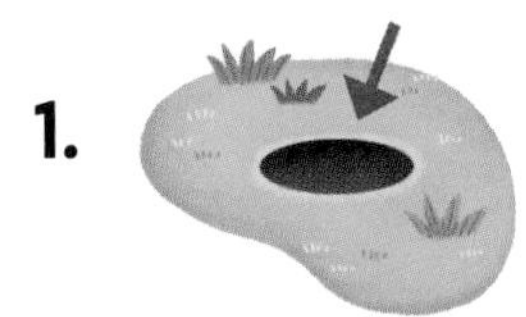 ole ➡ hole

2.  ole ➡ mole

3. 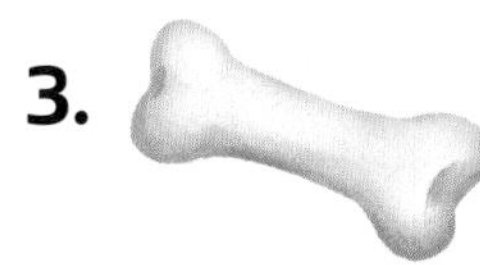 one ➡ bone

4. 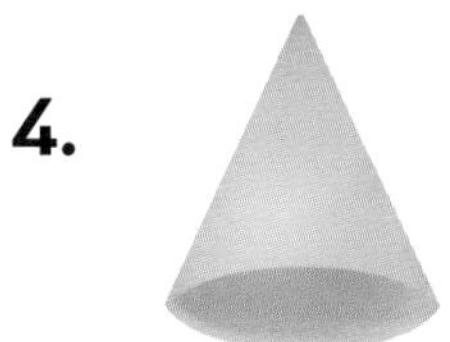 one ➡ cone

5. 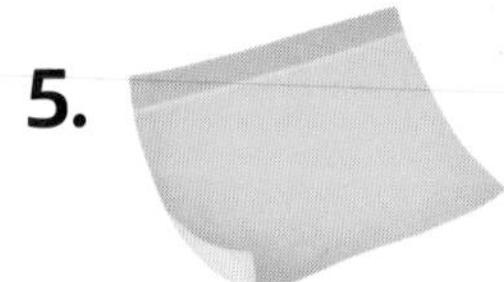 ote ➡ note

6.  ote ➡ vote

➡ Go to the workbook p. 24

Unit 07

Long Vowel u

Listen and repeat. 46

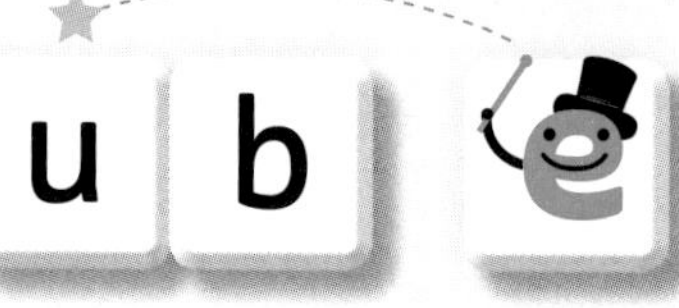

u b e

c u b e

u l e

m u l e

u t e

c u t e

A Read step by step.

1.

c

u b e

c u b e

2.

m

u l e

m u l e

3.

c

u t e

c u t e

B Read and say. 47

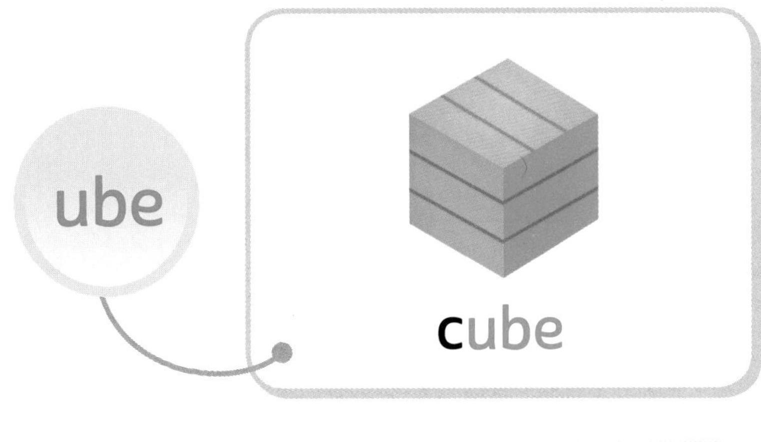
ube

cube

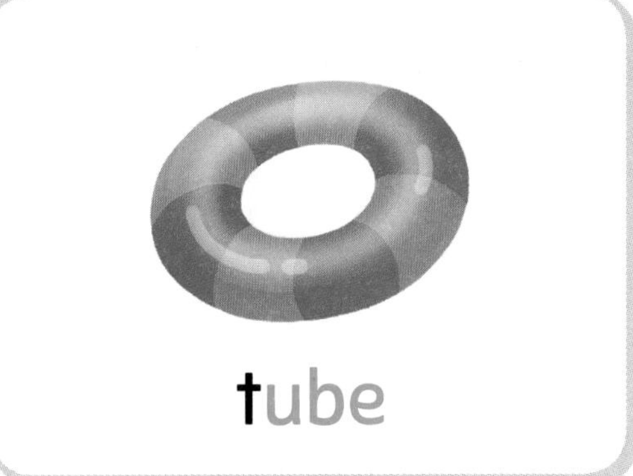

tube

ule

mule

rule

ute

cute

mute

C Point and chant. 48

ube ule ute

Listen and stick. 

49

1.

m
ute

2.
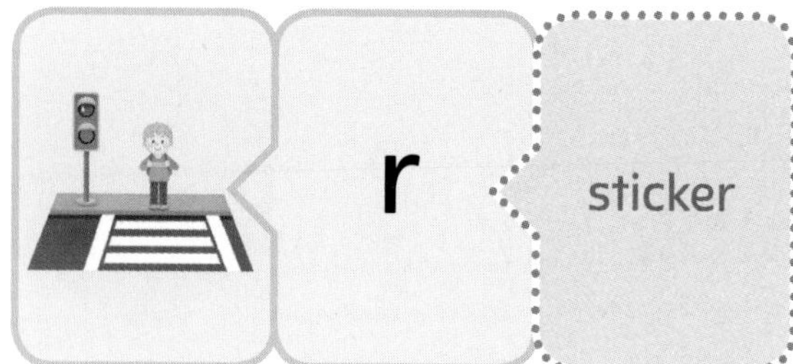
r
sticker

3.
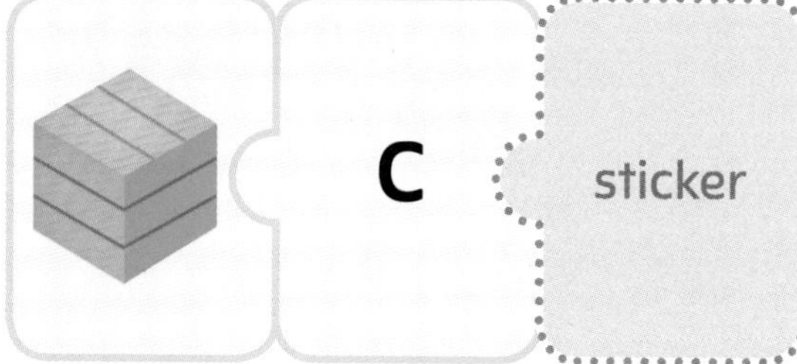
c
sticker

4.

m
sticker

5.

t
sticker

6.
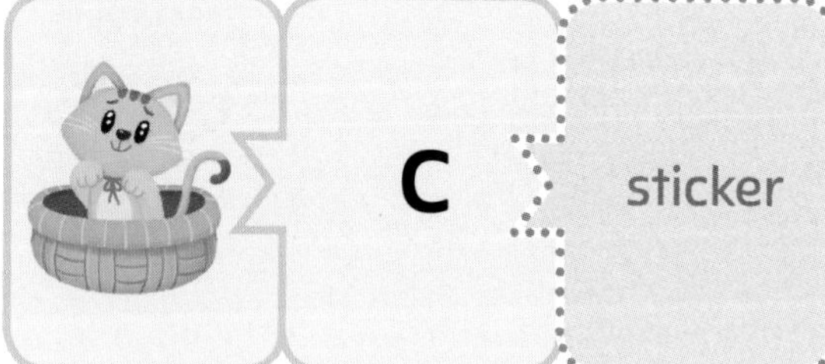
c
sticker

Say aloud. ❶ ❷ ❸

B Match and write.

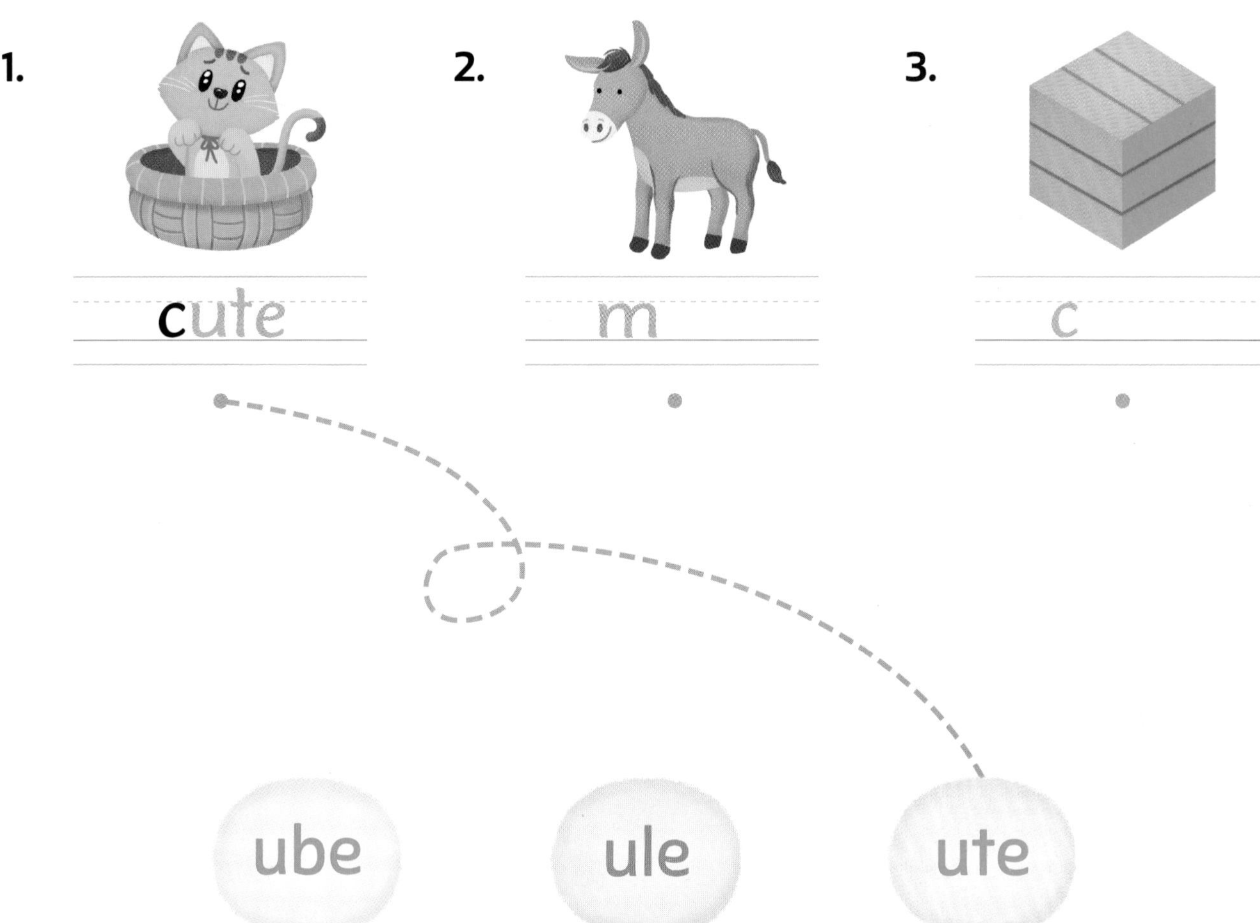
1.
cute
2.
m
3.
c
ube
ule
ute

4. r
5. m
6. t

Listen, circle and check.

1.

rule ☐
mule ☐

2.

cute ☐
mute ☐

3.

cube ☐
tube ☐

B Listen and circle.

1. 

The (rule / mule) is mute.

2. 

A cute doll is in the (cube / tube).

3. 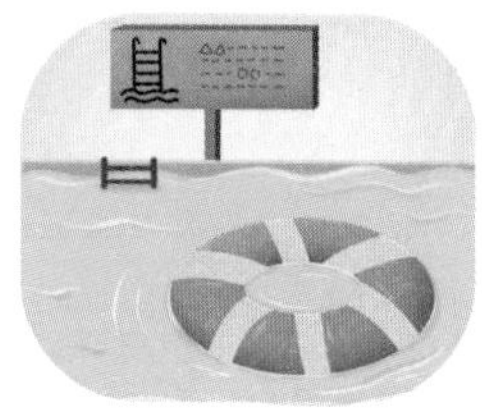

Keep the rules to use the (tube / cube).

C Read and find.

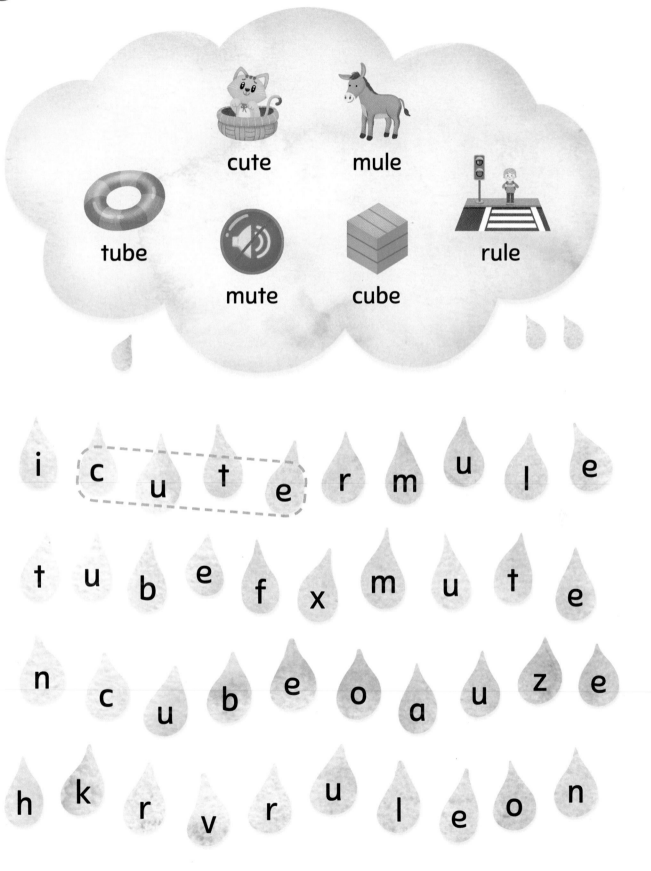

cute mule

tube rule

mute cube

i c u t e r m u l e

t u b e f x m u t e

n c u b e o a u z e

h k r v r u l e o n

Story Time

Let's read together. 52

The ant is on the tube.
She wears a cute hat.

The mule dives into the water.

The ant is wet.
The cute hat is wet, too.

The ant is in the cube.
She is happy now.

Sight Words

she into too now

Write and say.

1.  ube ➡ cube

2.  ube  tube

3.  ule  mule

4.  ule  rule

5.  ute 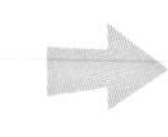 cute

6.  ute  mute

➡ Go to the workbook p. 28

Unit
08

Long Vowel u

- **Listen and repeat.** 53

u g e

h u g e

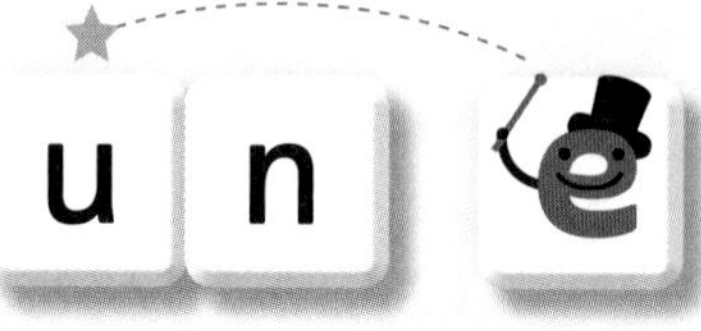

u n e

d u n e

u s e

f u s e

A Read step by step.

1.

h

u g e

h u g e

2.

d

u n e

d u n e

3.

f

u s e

f u s e

B Read and say. 54

uge

huge

une

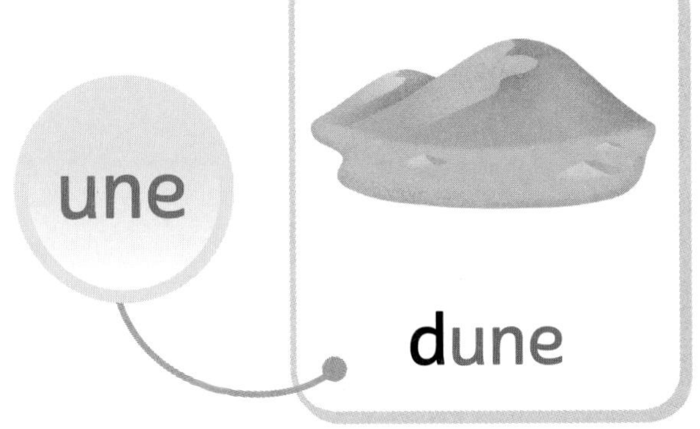

dune

6
1 2 3 4 5 6
7 8 9 10 11 12 13
14 15 16 17 18 19 20
21 22 23 24 25 26 27
28 29 30

June

tune

use

use

fuse

C Point and chant. 55

uge une use

Listen and check. 56

1. 

t
- use ☐
- une ☑

2. 

f
- uge ☐
- use ☐

3. 

h
- uge ☐
- une ☐

4. 

d
- use ☐
- une ☐

5. 

J
- use ☐
- une ☐

6. 

- use ☐
- uge ☐

Say aloud. ❶ ❷ ❸

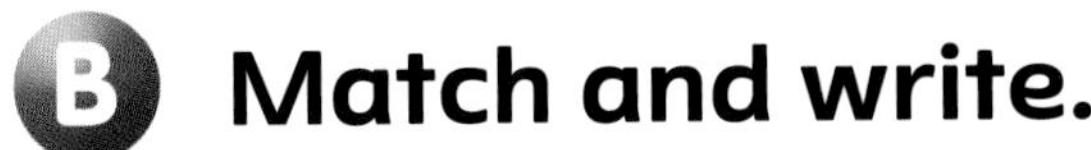

B Match and write.

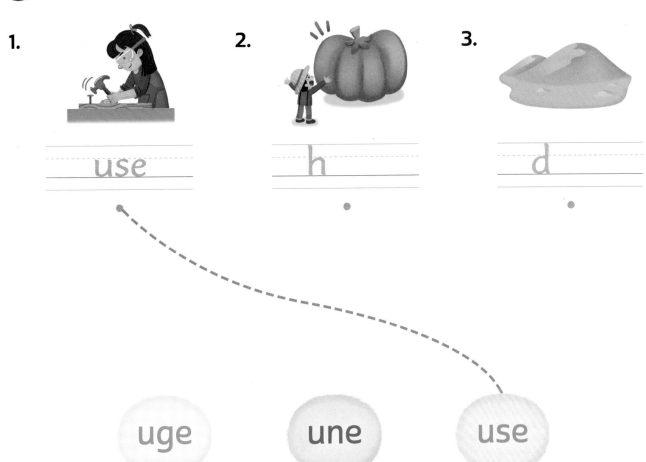

1. use
2. h
3. d

uge une use

4. J
5. f
6. t

A Listen, circle and color. 57

1.

J s u e f n

2.

d s u e h g

3.

t n u e h g

4.

f s u e d n

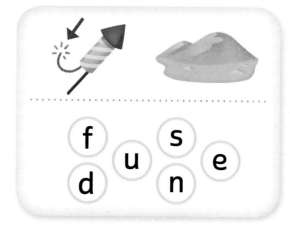

B Listen and circle. 58

1. I dance to a tune on the (use / dune).

2. A huge bear has a (tune / fuse).

3. I use a fan in (June / huge).

C Read and find.

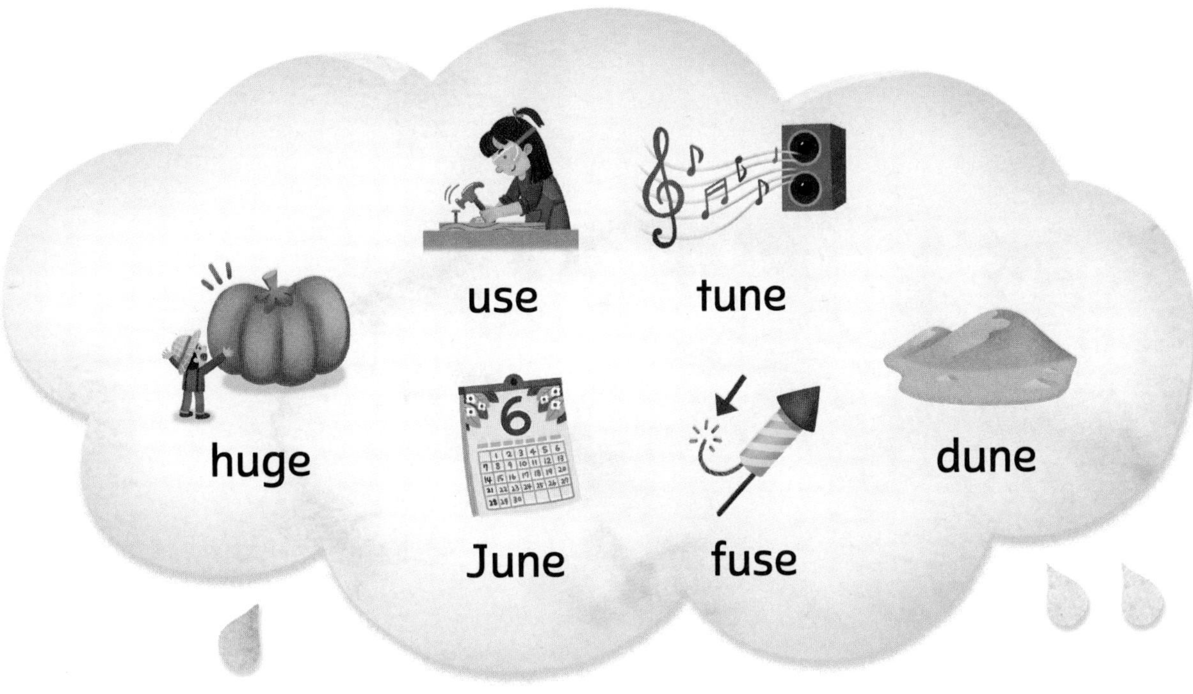
use
tune
huge
dune
June
fuse

k n u s e h t u n e

y h u g e m J u n e

t s u v e f u s e n

v n e d u n e w t e

Story Time

Let's read together. 59

Meg is on the dune.
It is very cold.

Meg finds a case and a key. A tune plays.

Meg uses the key.
A huge house comes out.

It is warm in the house.

Sight Words

cold finds out warm

Write and say.

1. 
uge ➡ huge

2. 
une ➡ dune

3. 
une ➡ June

4. une ➡ tune

5. 
use ➡ use

6. 
use ➡ fuse

➡ Go to the workbook p. 32

Unit 09

Long Vowel ea, ee

Listen and repeat. 60

ea

s ea

ee

b ee

A Read step by step.

1. ea

s ea

2. ee

b ee

B Read and say. 61

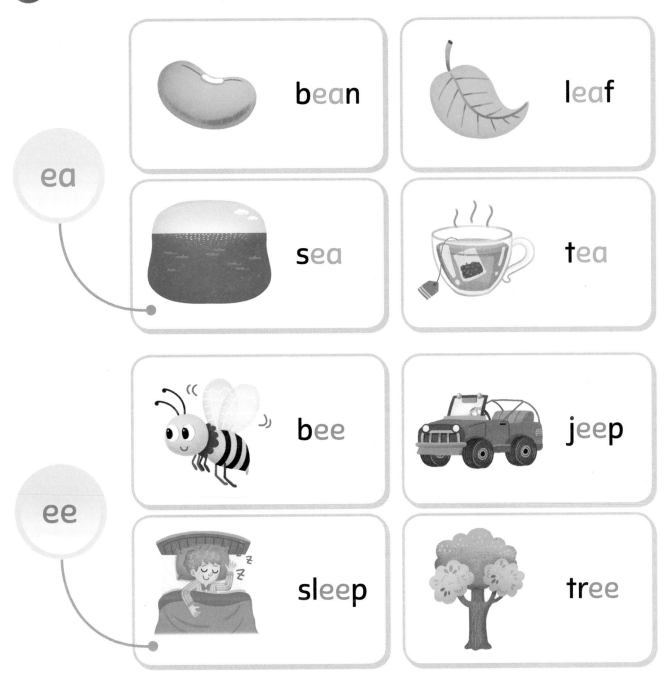

ea

bean

leaf

sea

tea

ee

bee

jeep

sleep

tree

C Point and chant. 62

ea

ee

A Listen and check. 63

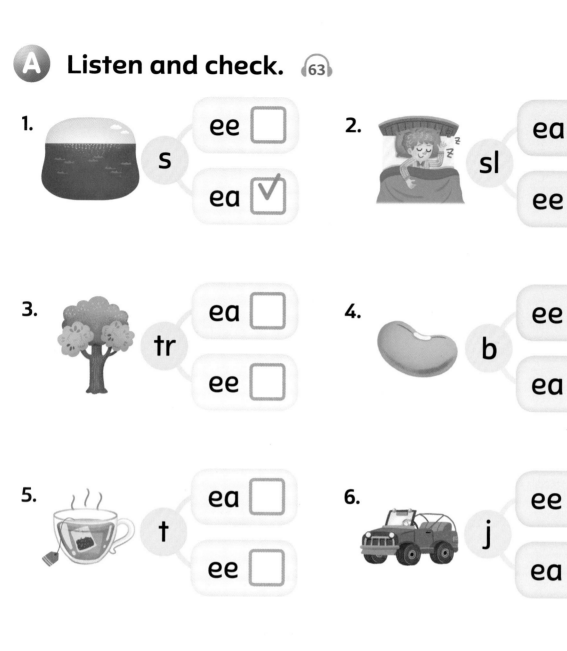

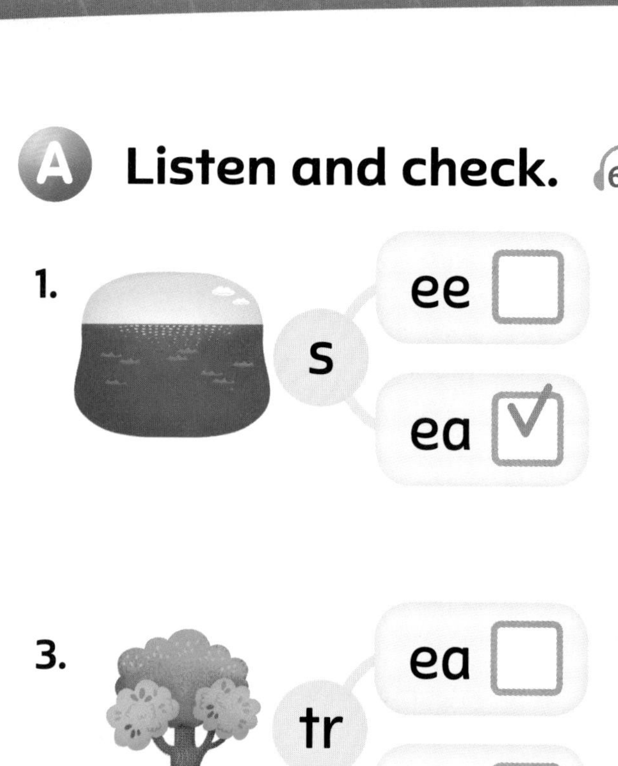

1. s — ee ☐ / ea ☑
2. sl _ p — ea ☐ / ee ☐
3. tr — ea ☐ / ee ☐
4. b _ n — ee ☐ / ea ☐
5. t — ea ☐ / ee ☐
6. j _ p — ee ☐ / ea ☐
7. b — ee ☐ / ea ☐
8. l _ f — ea ☐ / ee ☐

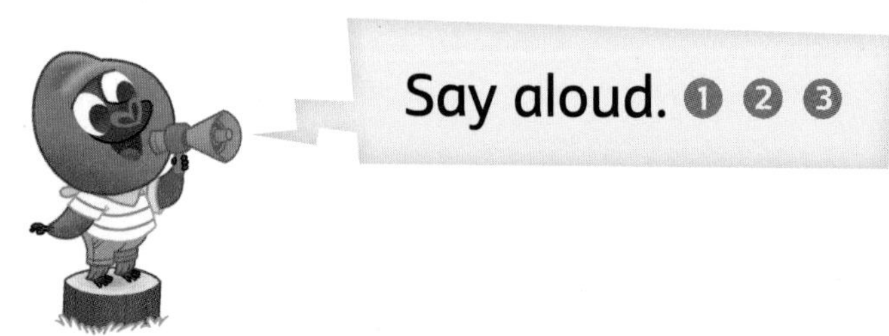
Say aloud. ❶ ❷ ❸

B Match and write.

1. 
tree

2. 
t

3. 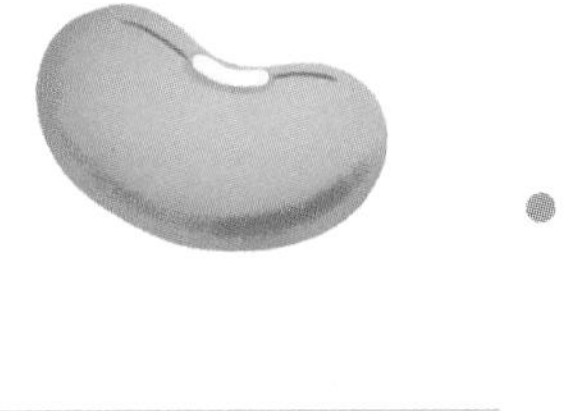
b n

4. 
j p

ea

5. 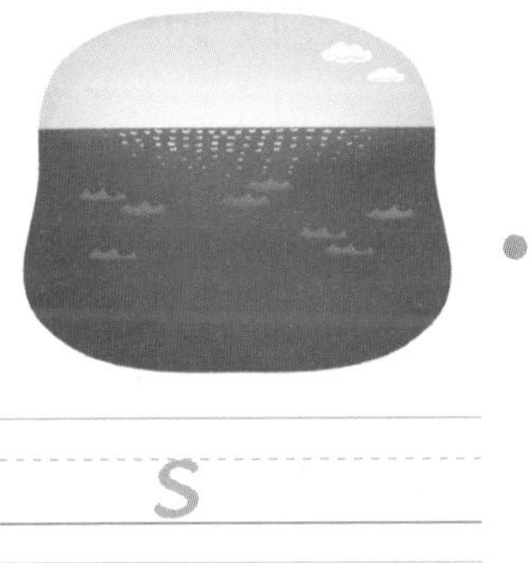
s

6. 
sl p

ee

7. 
l f

8. 
b

A Listen, circle and check. 64

1.   

bean ☐
leaf ☐

2.   

sea ☐
tea ☐

3.   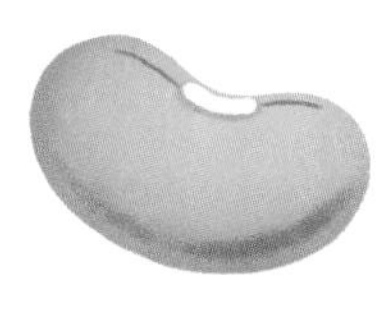

jeep ☐
sleep ☐

B Listen and circle. 65

1. 

I drink tea by the (tree / bee).

2. 

A bee is on the (sea / leaf).

3. 

The dogs sleep in the (jeep / tree).

C Read and find.

tea

tree

leaf

bee

a	b	o	s	e	a	e	w
l	t	e	b	u	f	h	c
h	e	v	a	e	s	s	i
q	a	a	y	n	e	l	f
z	e	a	f	n	i	e	k
t	j	e	e	p	v	e	d
m	f	t	r	e	e	p	r

sea

sleep

jeep

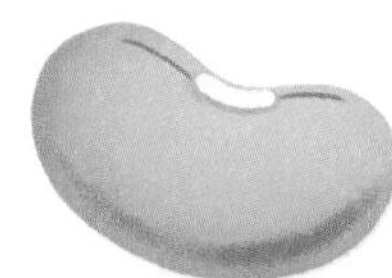
bean

Story Time

Let's read together. 66

The bean is on the leaf.
The bean makes tea.
The monkey sleeps under the tree.

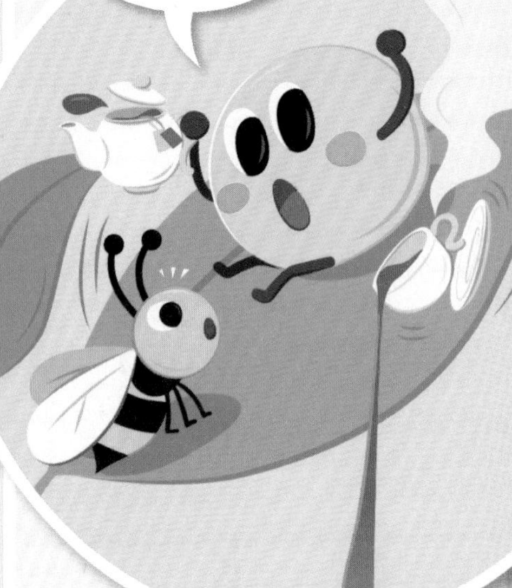
Oh, no!

The bee sits on the leaf.
The tea spills.

The monkey hops and hops.

Sight Words

makes under sits and

Writing Time

Write and say.

1. 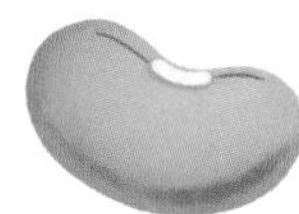 ea ➡ bean

2.  ea ➡ leaf

3.  ea  sea

4.  ea  tea

5.  ee 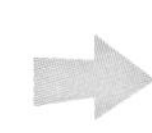 bee

6.  ee  jeep

7.  ee  sleep

8.  ee  tree

➡ Go to the workbook p. 36

Unit
10

Long Vowel ai, ay

Listen and repeat. 67

ai

m ai l

g r ay

A Read step by step.

1.

ai

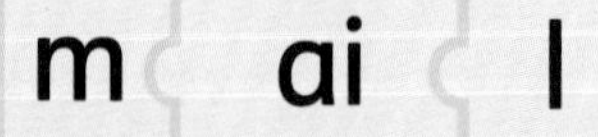
m ai l

2.

ay

g r ay

B Read and say. 68

ai

mail

nail

rain

train

ay

day

gray

hay

tray

C Point and chant. 69

ai
ay

A Listen and check. 70

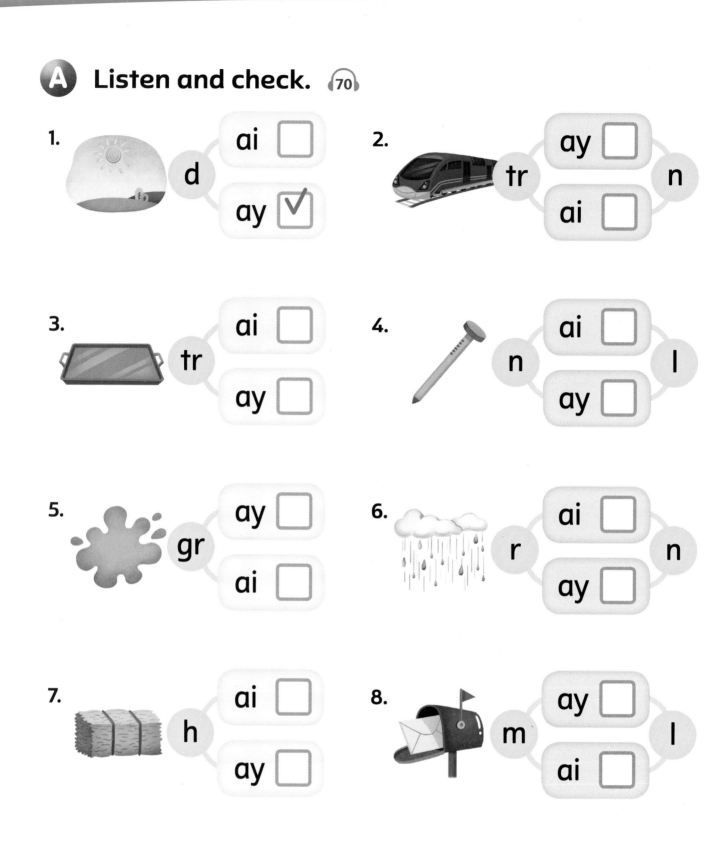

1.  d — ai ☐ / ay ☑

2.  tr — ay ☐ / ai ☐ — n

3.  tr — ai ☐ / ay ☐

4.  n — ai ☐ / ay ☐ — l

5.  gr — ay ☐ / ai ☐

6.  r — ai ☐ / ay ☐ — n

7. 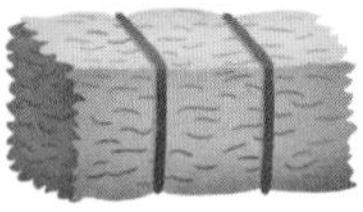 h — ai ☐ / ay ☐

8.  m — ay ☐ / ai ☐ — l

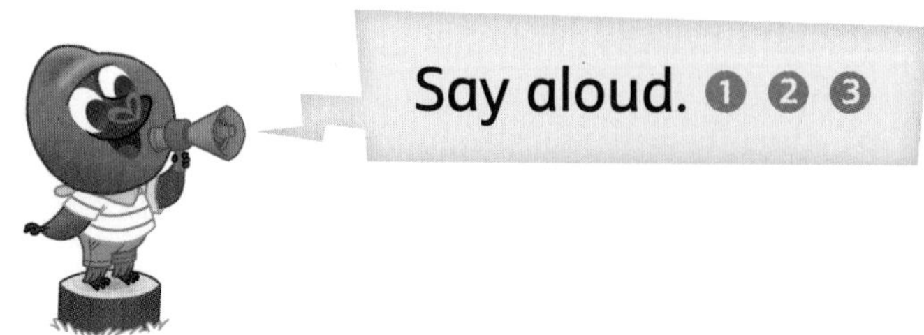
Say aloud. ❶ ❷ ❸

B Match and write.

1. 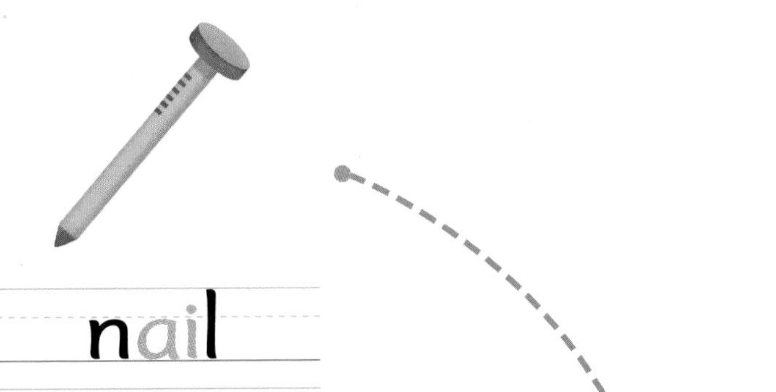

nail

2. 

h

3. 

gr

ai

4. 

tr n

5. 

m l

ay

6. 

tr

7. 

r n

8. 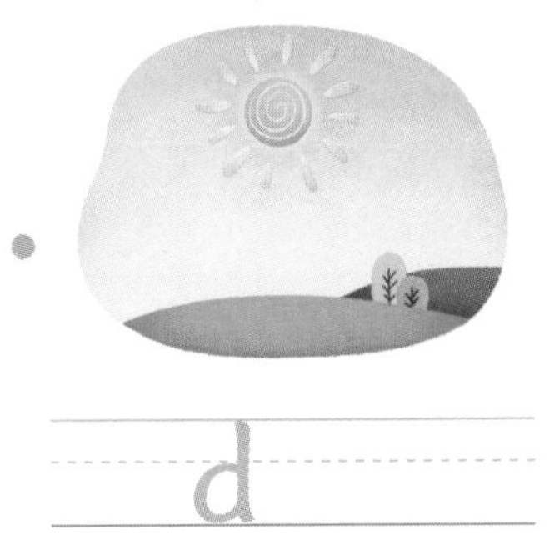

d

A Listen, circle and check. 71

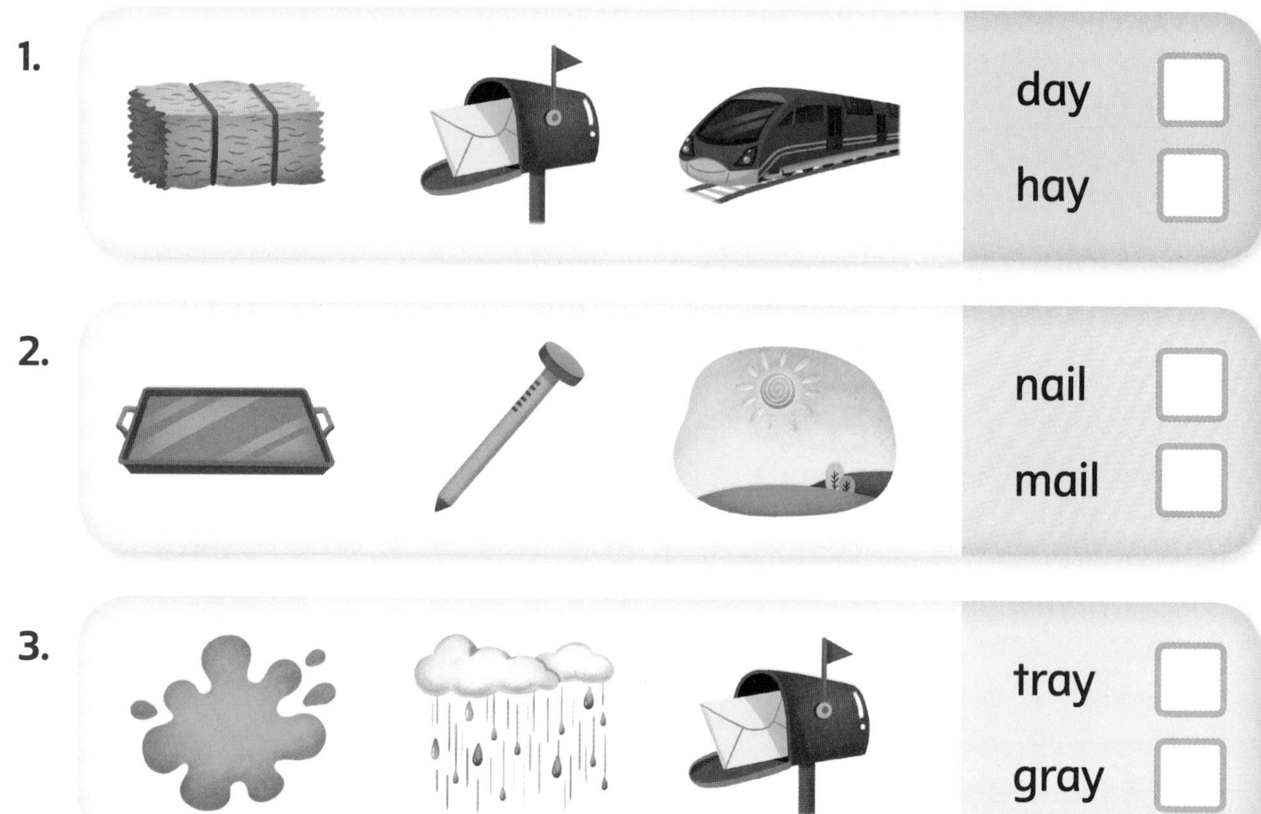

1. day ☐ hay ☐

2. nail ☐ mail ☐

3. tray ☐ gray ☐

B Listen and circle. 72

1. The (day / nail) is gray.

2. Hay is on the (tray / rain).

3. A (train / mail) runs in the rain.

C Read and find.

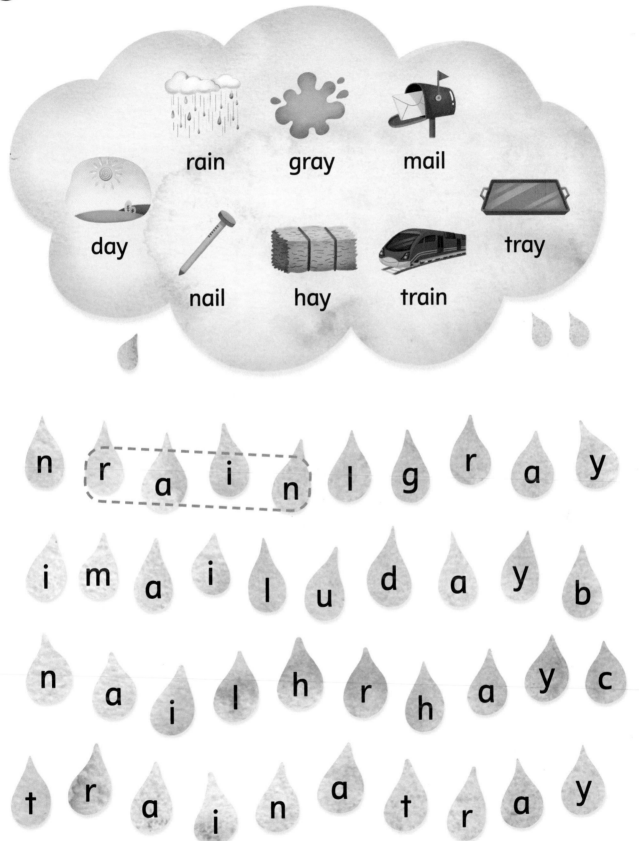

rain gray mail

day tray

nail hay train

n r a i n l g r a y

i m a i l u d a y b

n a i l h r h a y c

t r a i n a t r a y

Story Time

Let's read together. 73

This is Ben.
He cooks all day.

He puts pins and nails into the pan.

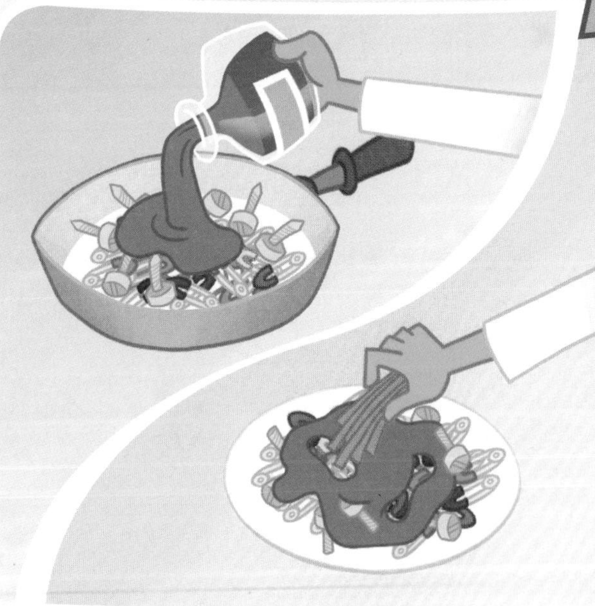

He adds gray ink.
He puts hay on the top.

Yummy!

He puts it on the tray.

Sight Words

this cooks all adds top

Write and say.

1. ai → mail

2.  ai → nail

3.  ai  rain

4.  ai  train

5.  ay 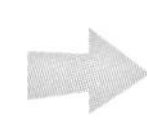 day

6.  ay  gray

7. 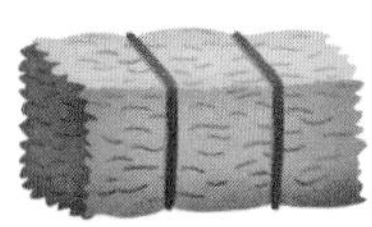 ay  hay

8.  ay  tray

➡ Go to the workbook p. 40

Review 2

A Listen and match. 74

1.

2.

3.

4.

ote

ule

ea

ay

5.

6.

7.

8.

B Look and number.

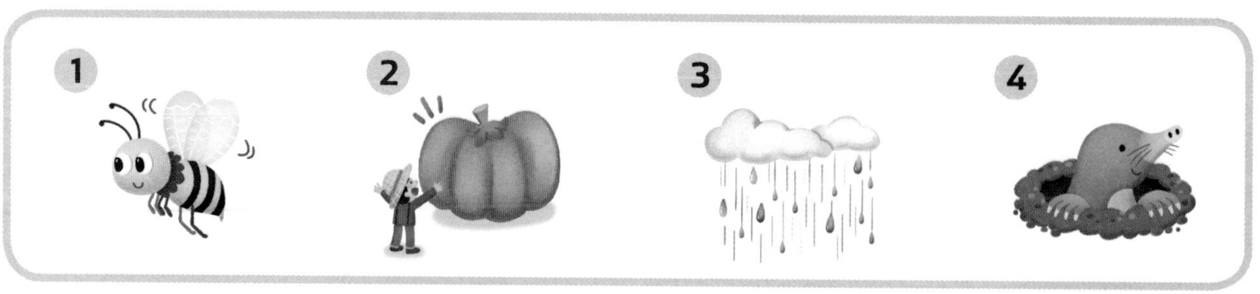

1. rain 3
2. mole
3. huge
4. bee

C Read and write.

June	bone	use	cute
~~jeep~~	train	hay	tune

1. jeep

2.

3.

4.

5.

6.

7.

8.

D Listen and color. (75)

1. d une ote
2. c ole ute
3. h ule ole
4. d ay ea

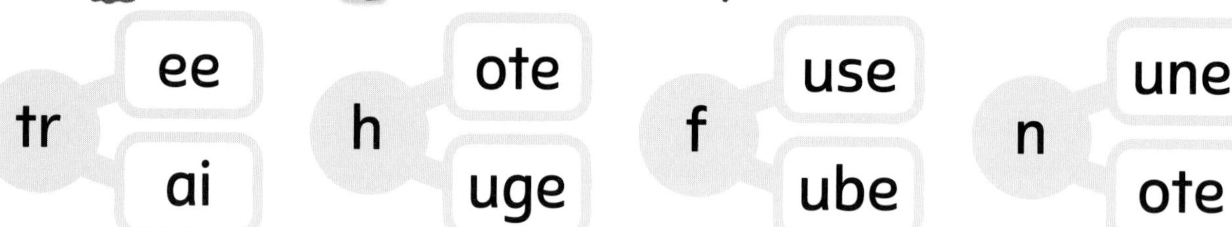

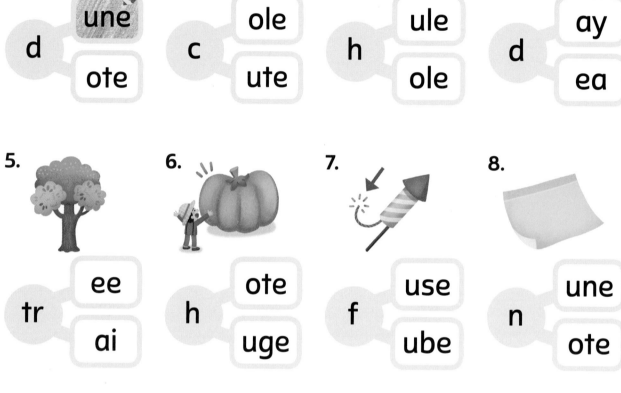

5. tr ee ai
6. h ote uge
7. f use ube
8. n une ote

E Circle and write.

1. ai ay
nail
2. ea ee
sl p
3. one ute
m

F Look and write.

tube	leaf	bone	mail
bean	cube	rain	cone

-one

bone

-ube

-ai-

-ea-

Phonics Words

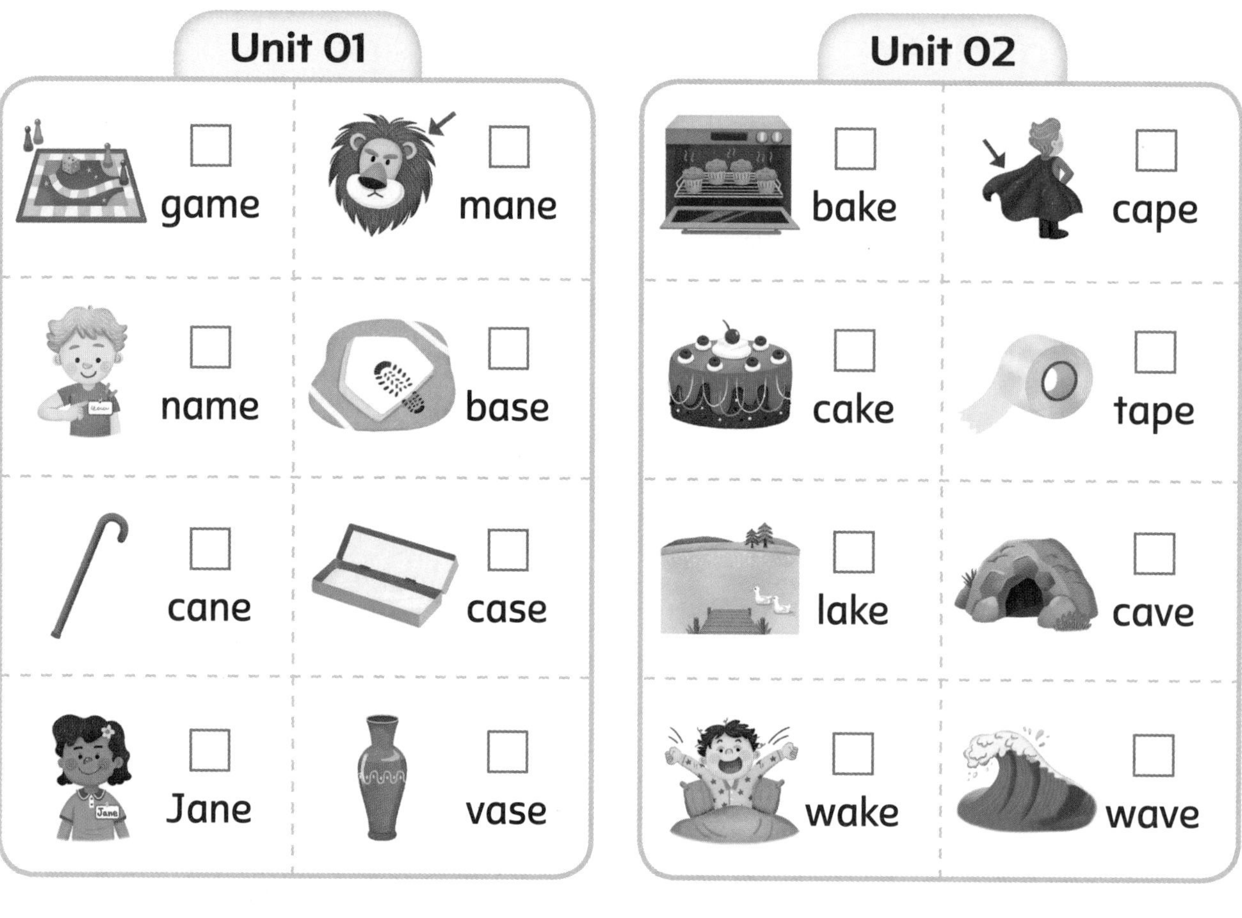
Unit 01
game
mane
name
base
cane
case
Jane
vase
Unit 02
bake
cape
cake
tape
lake
cave
wake
wave

Unit 03

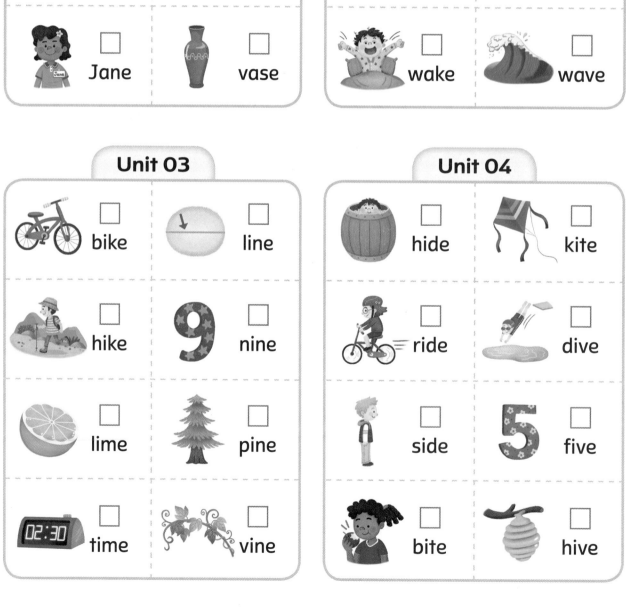

bike	line
hike	nine
lime	pine
time	vine

Unit 04

hide	kite
ride	dive
side	five
bite	hive

Unit 05

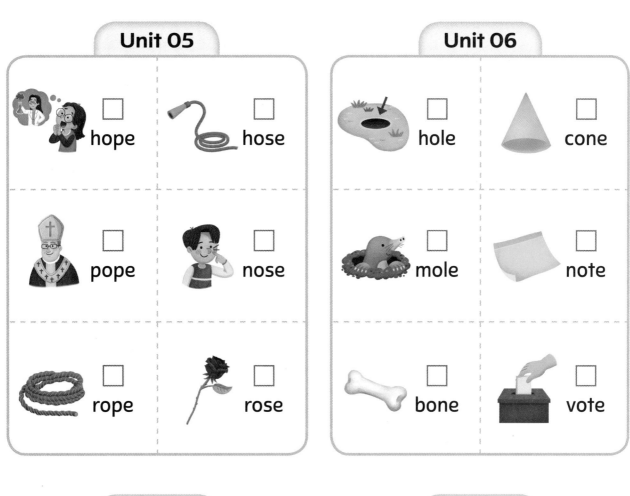

☐ hope	☐ hose
☐ pope	☐ nose
☐ rope	☐ rose

Unit 06

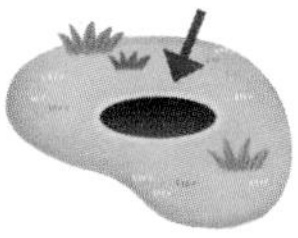

☐ hole	☐ cone
☐ mole	☐ note
☐ bone	☐ vote

Unit 07

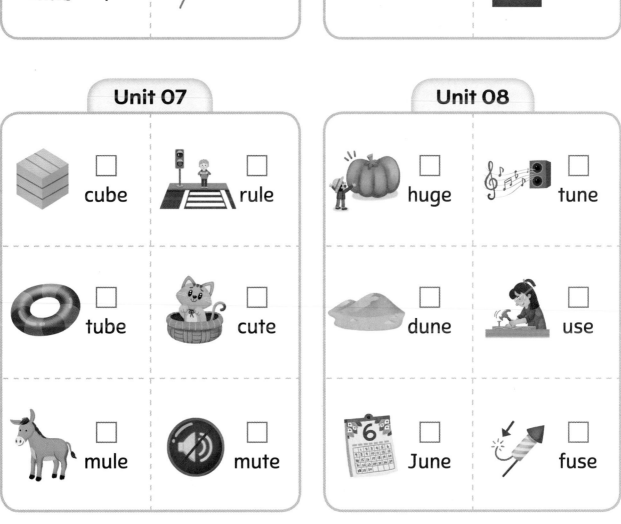

☐ cube	☐ rule
☐ tube	☐ cute
☐ mule	☐ mute

Unit 08

☐ huge	☐ tune
☐ dune	☐ use
☐ June	☐ fuse

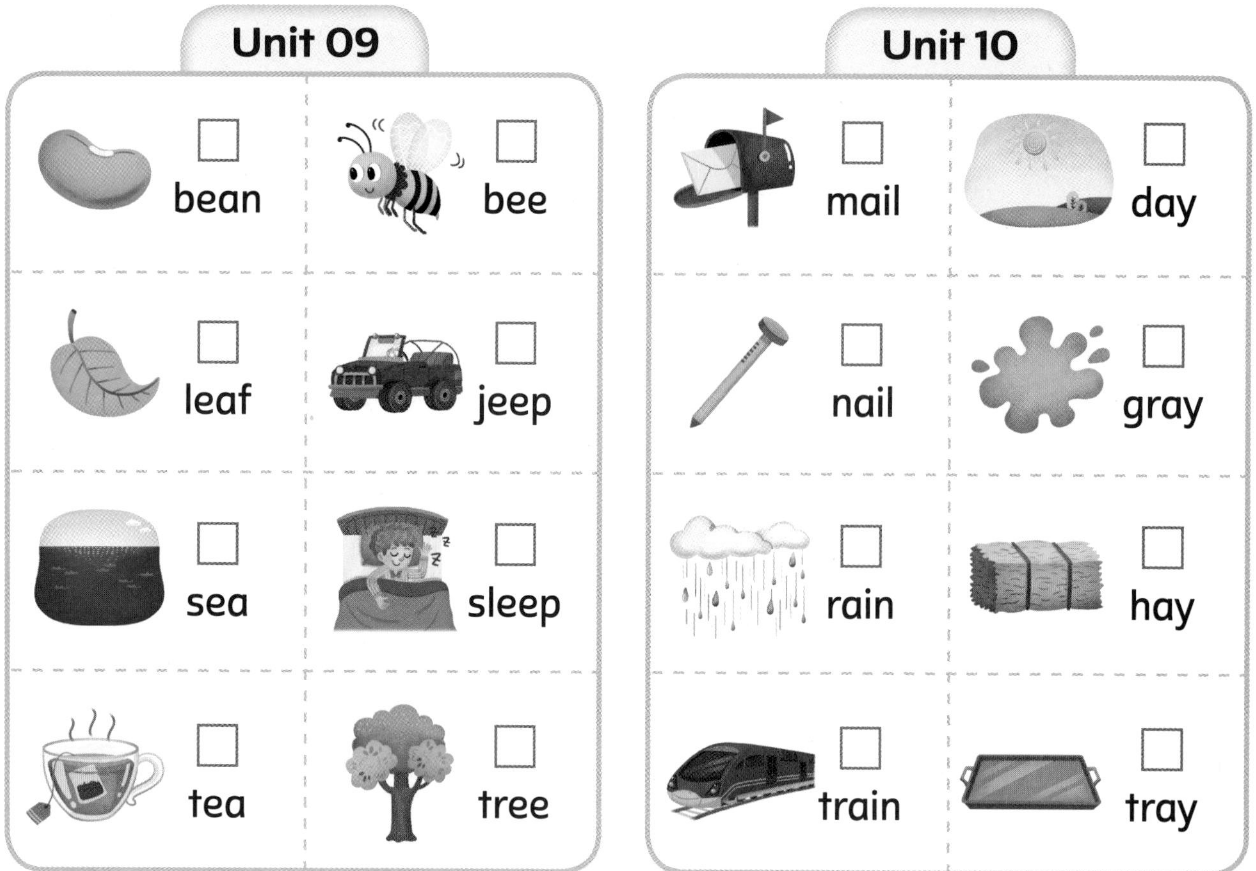
Unit 09
bean
bee
leaf
jeep
sea
sleep
tea
tree
Unit 10
mail
day
nail
gray
rain
hay
train
tray

• Sight Words

Unit 01	sees	can	open	my	
Unit 02	help	is	on	thank	
Unit 03	you	they're	no	not	
Unit 04	has	finds	puts	water	
Unit 05	very	hot	comes	gets	
Unit 06	looks	falls	gives		
Unit 07	she	into	too	now	
Unit 08	cold	finds	out	warm	
Unit 09	makes	under	sits	and	
Unit 10	this	cooks	all	adds	top

Let's Go to the English World
Phonics

Readers 3

The Fox and a Cake

76

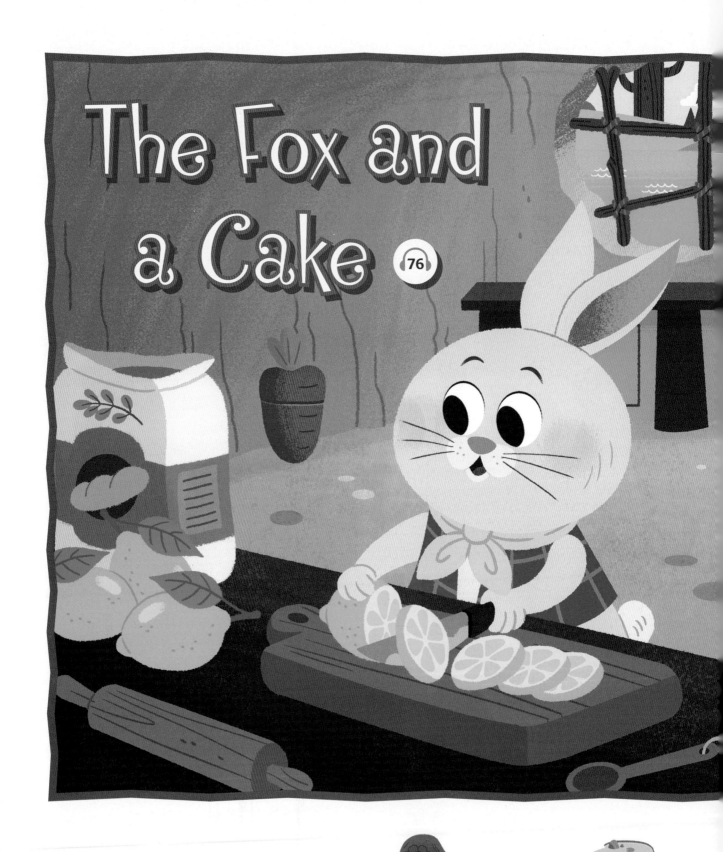

The rabbits live in a cave by the lake.

They bake a lime cake.

“This cake is mine.”

“No, it’s mine, Jane.”

The fox with a cane comes.

He draws a line on the cake.

"Oh, this side is bigger."

The fox bites the cake.

"Now, this side is bigger."

Bye, bye!

The fox eats all of the cake.

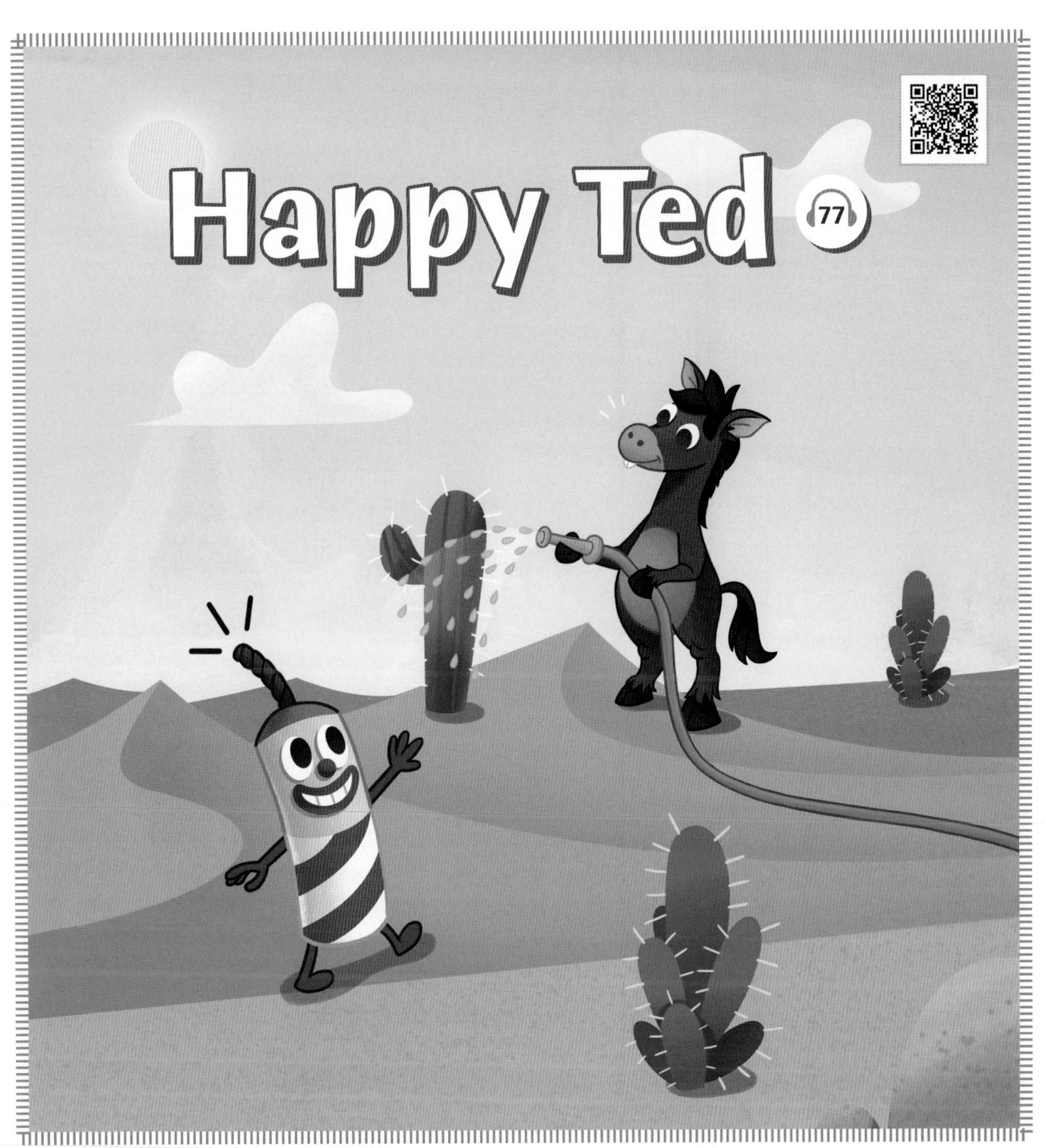
Happy Ted
77

Ted has a fuse.

He sees a mule on the dune.

He wants to help the mule.

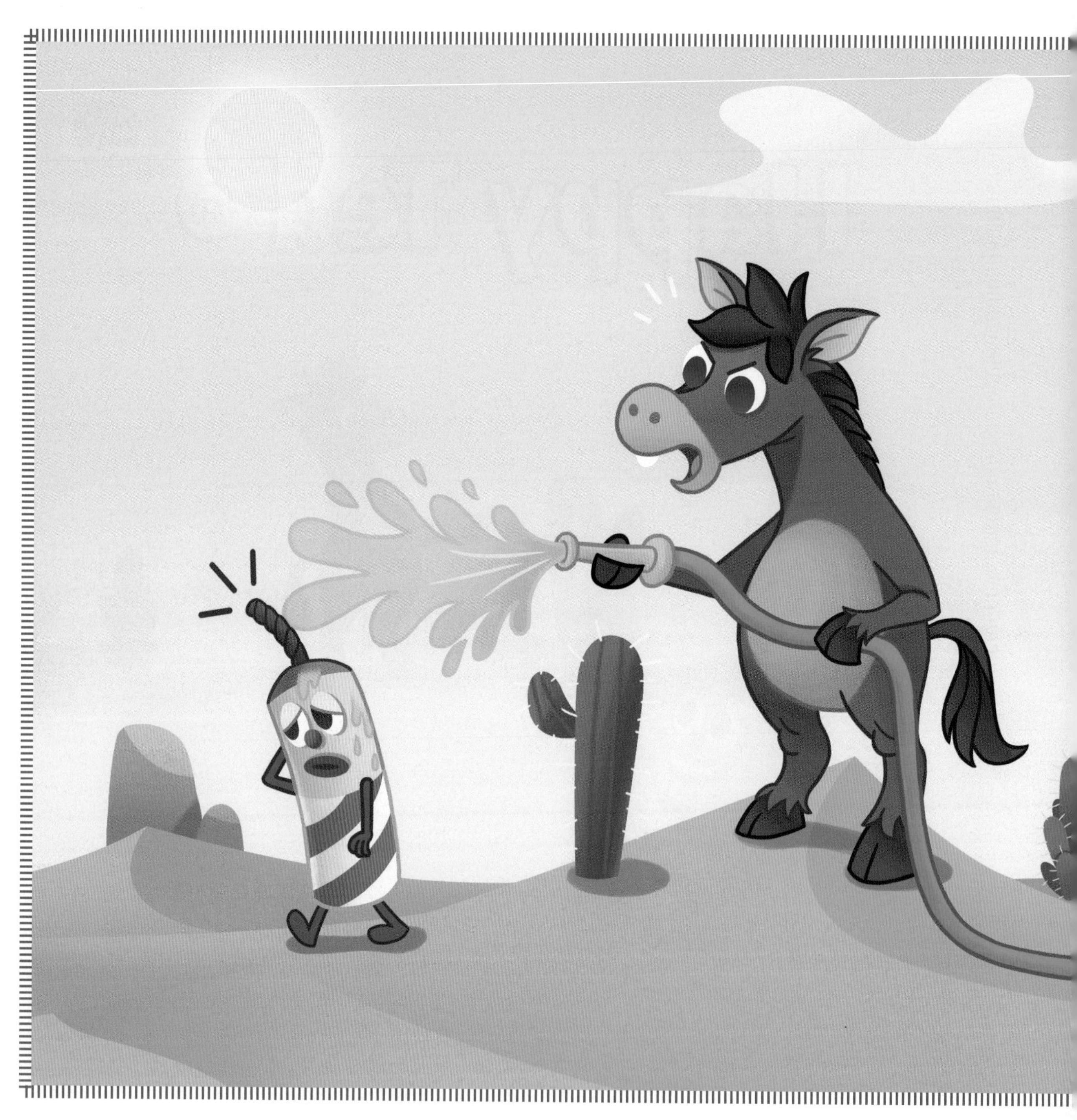

The mule has a hose.

The mule says, "Go away!"

Ted is sad.

A mole is on the tube.

The mole says, “Go away!”

Ted is sad.

Happy Birthday

Ted sees cute ants with cone hats.

He wants to help them.

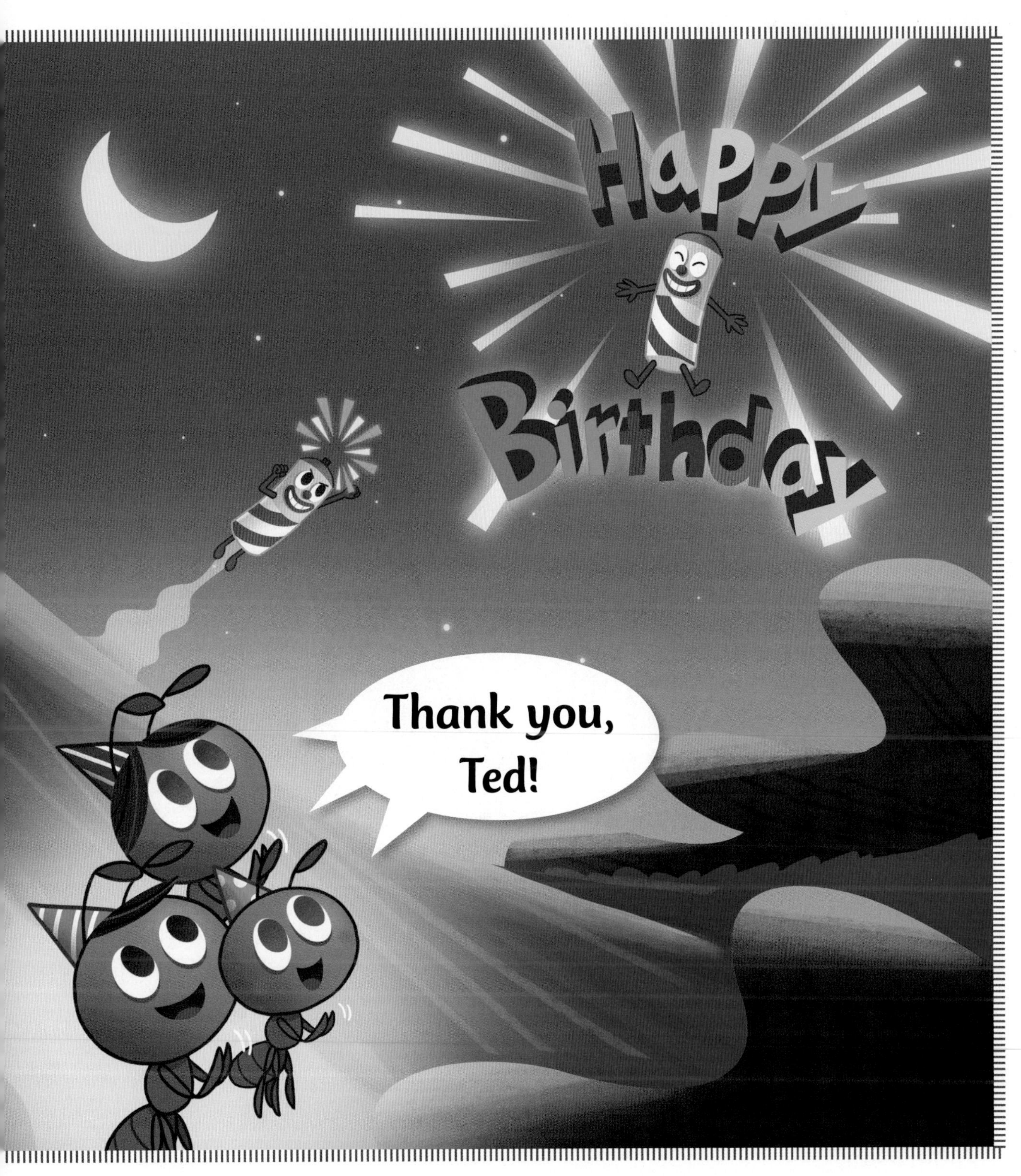
Happy Birthday
Thank you, Ted!

The ants like Ted.

Ted is happy now.

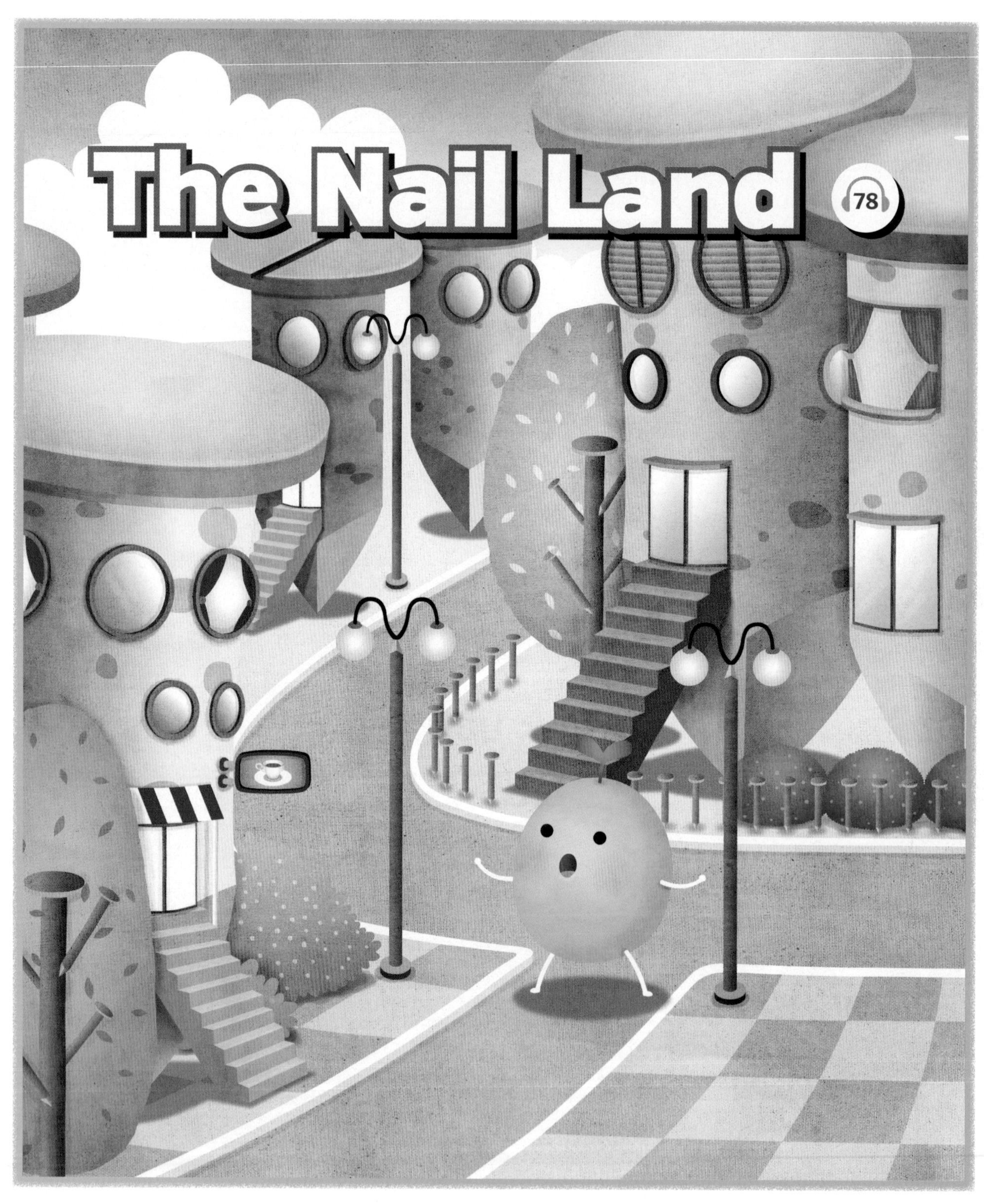
The Nail Land
78

The bean is in the nail land.

The nails are gray.

Z Z Z

The bean sees a nail house.

The dog sleeps in the house.

Come and have some tea.

The bees sit around the nail table.

The bee brings tea and cake on a tray.

Nail rain falls down.

"Help me!"

Thank you!

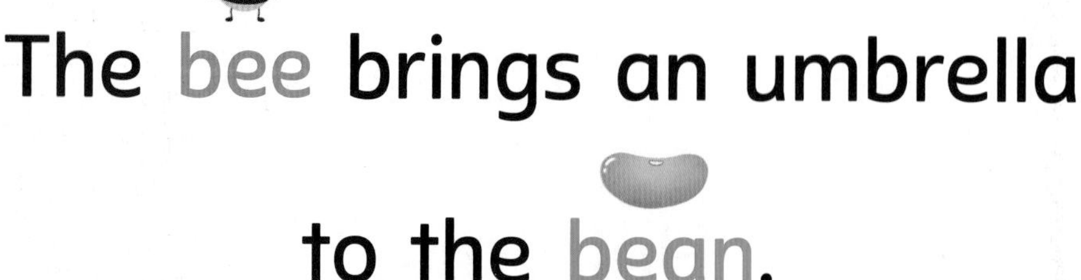

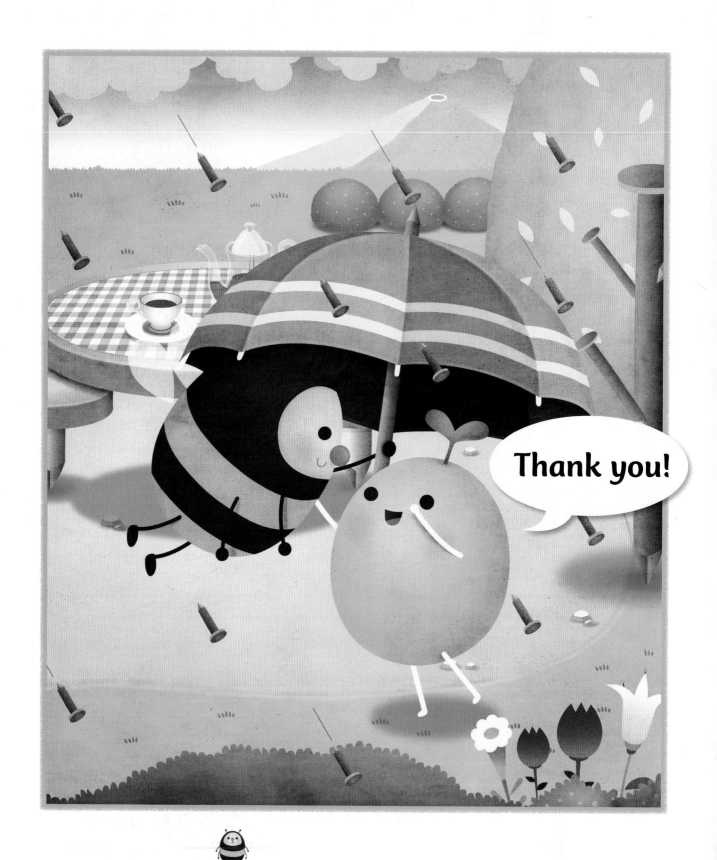

The bee brings an umbrella

to the bean.

1

2

3

4

Jane

5

6
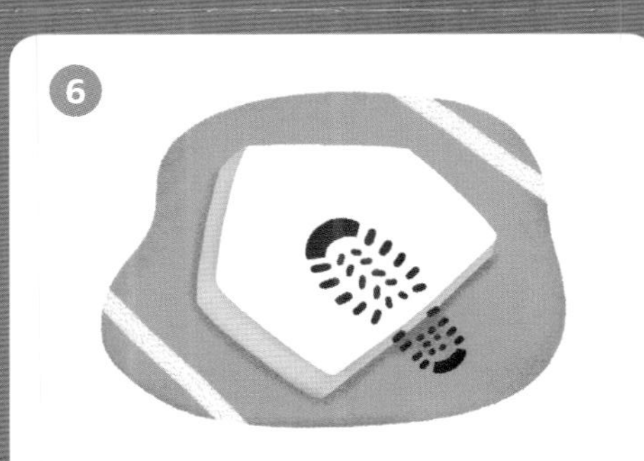

7
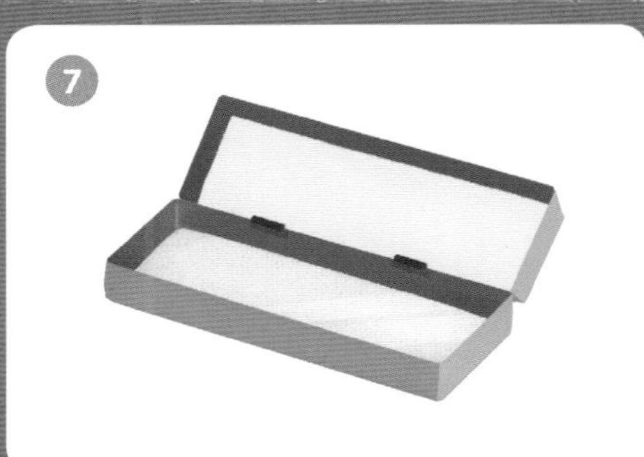

8
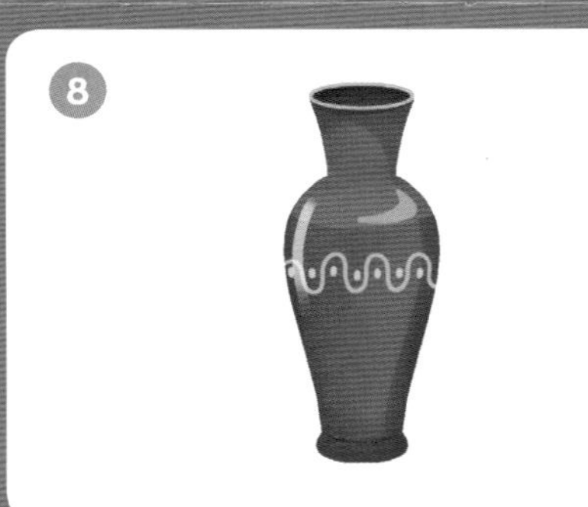

9

10
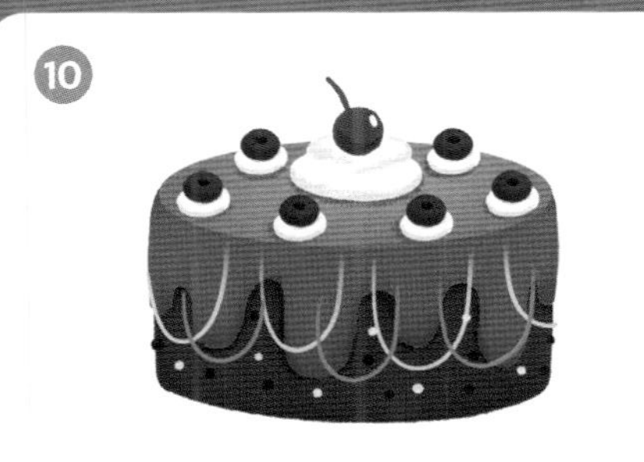

11

12

13

14
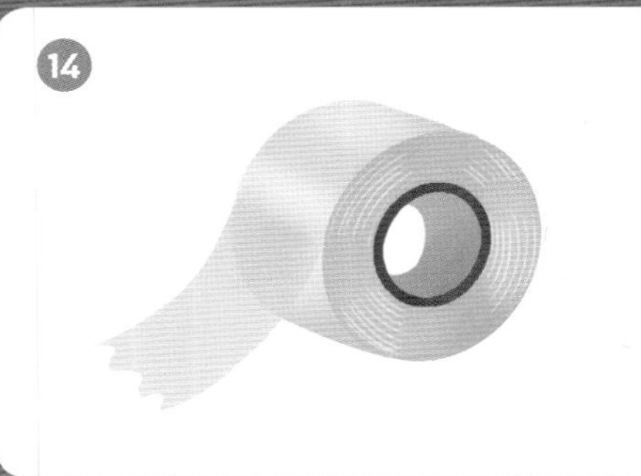

15

16

Jane	cane	name	game
vase	case	base	mane
wake	lake	cake	bake
wave	cave	tape	cape

17

18

19

20

02:30

21
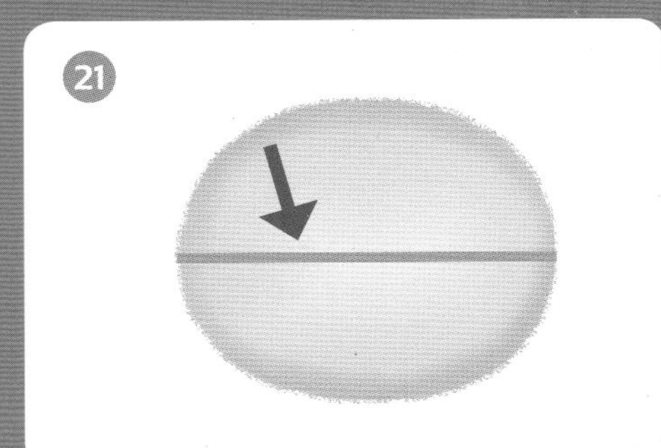

22

23
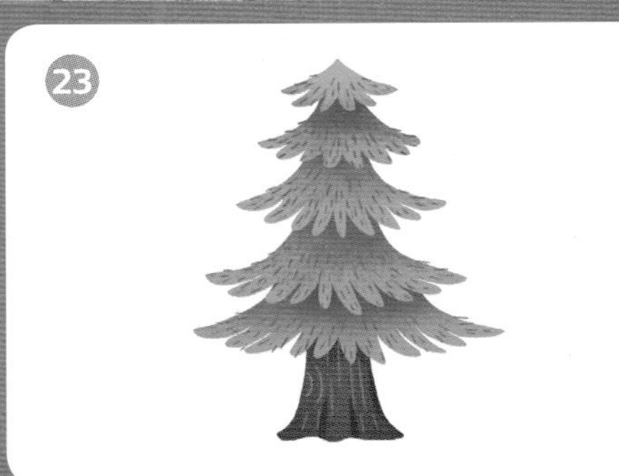

24

25

26

27

28

29
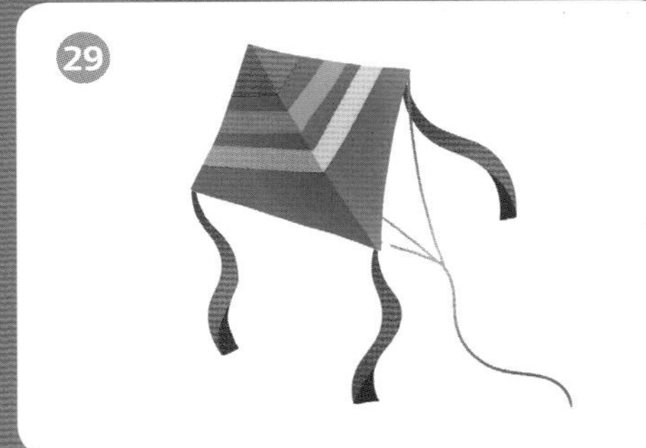

30

31

32
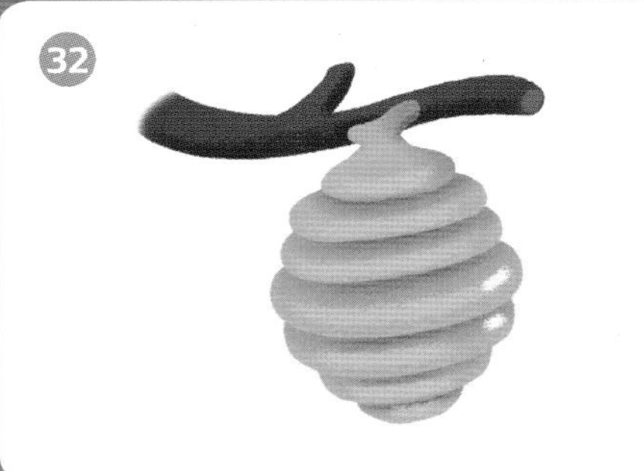

time	lime	hike	bike
vine	pine	nine	line
bite	side	ride	hide
hive	five	dive	kite

33

34

35

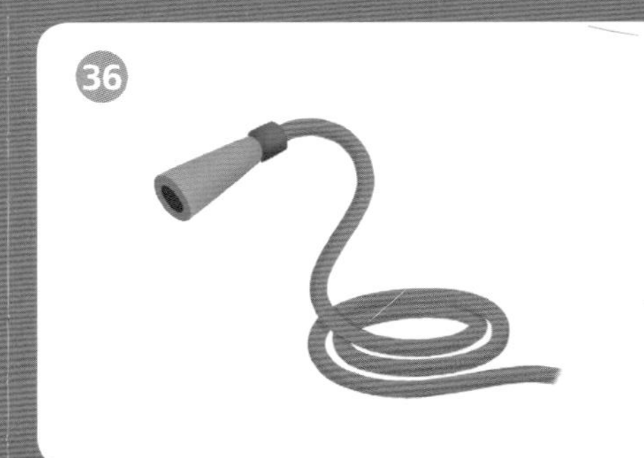
36

37

38

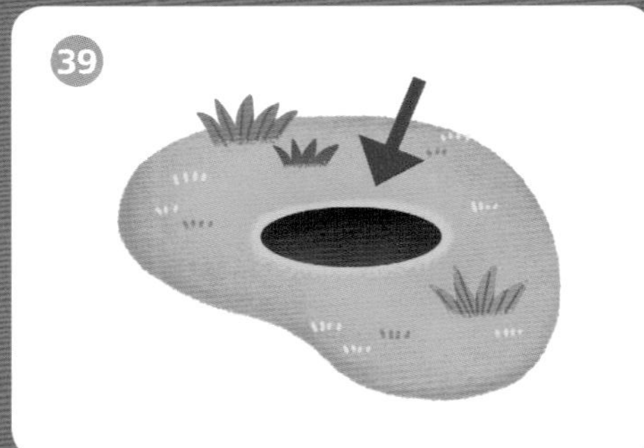
39

40

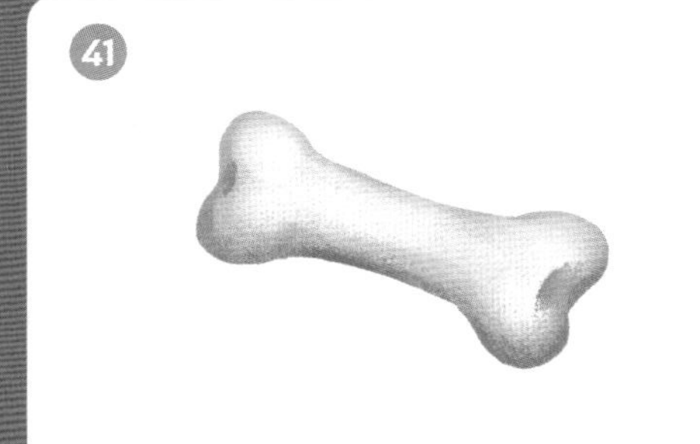
41

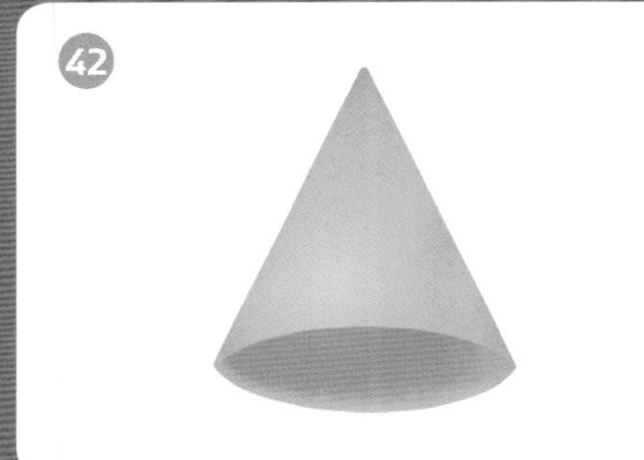
42

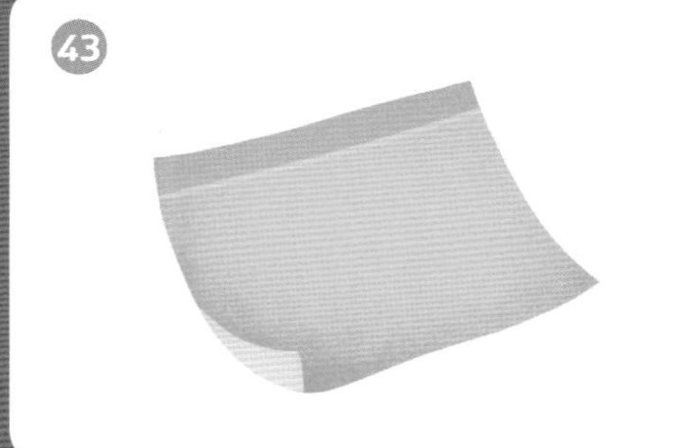
43

44

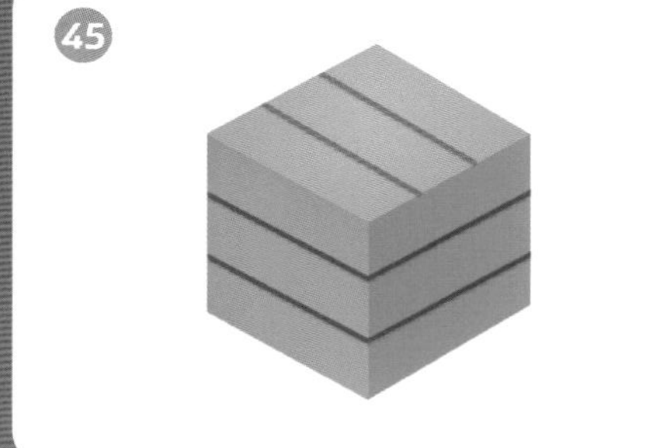
45

46

47

48

hose	rope	pope	hope
mole	hole	rose	nose
vote	note	cone	bone
rule	mule	tube	cube

49

50

51

52

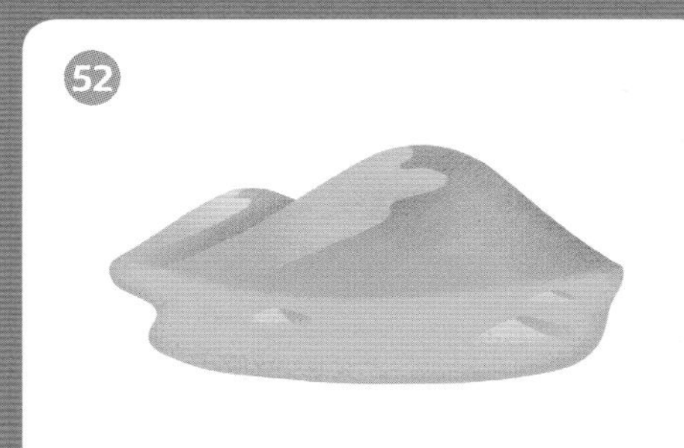

53

54

55

56

57

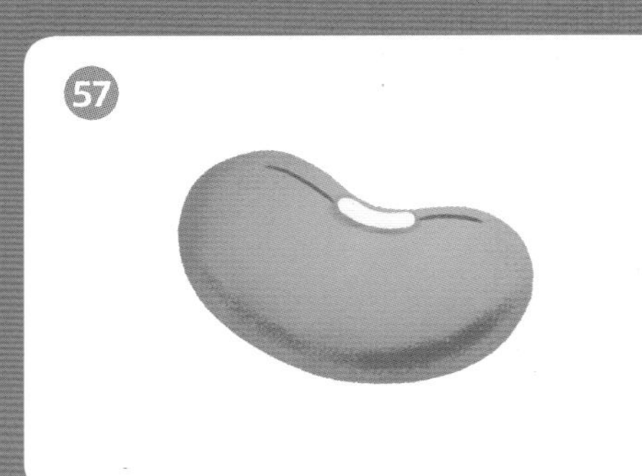

58

59

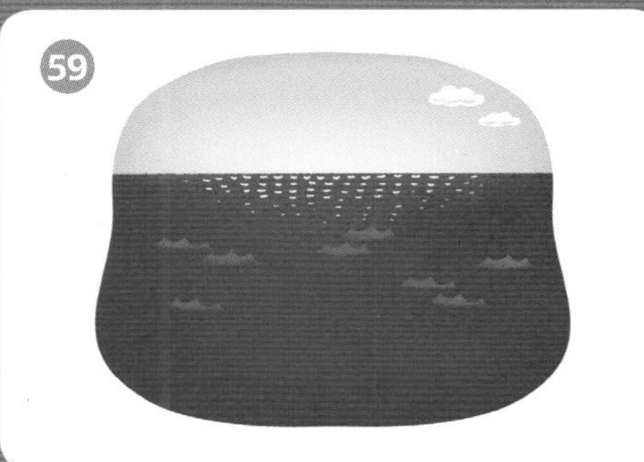

60

61

62

63

64

dune	huge	mute	cute
fuse	use	tune	June
tea	sea	leaf	bean
tree	sleep	jeep	bee

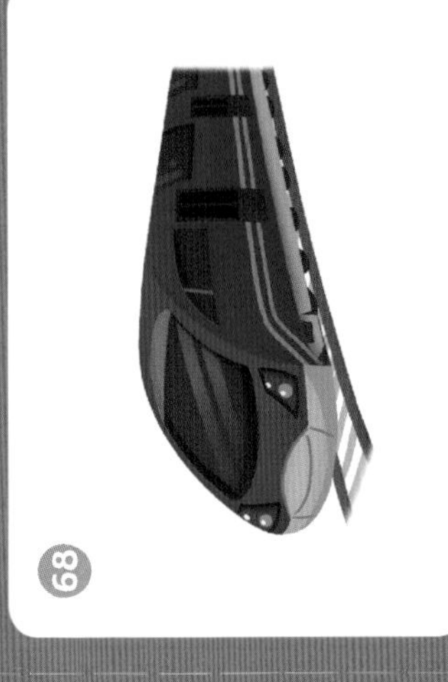
68
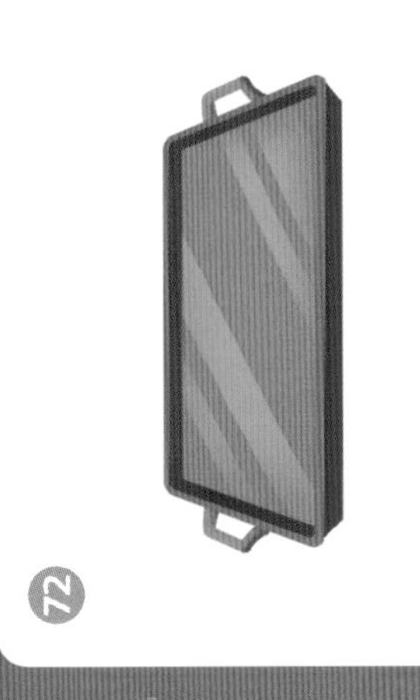
72

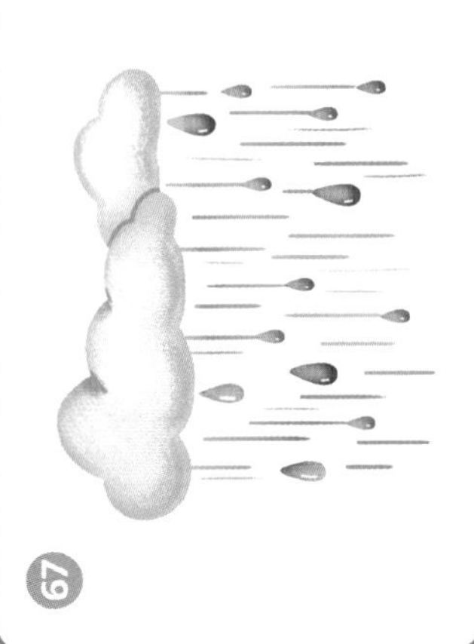
67
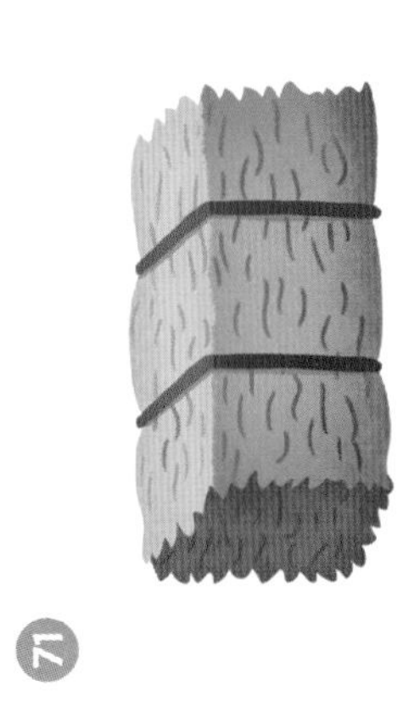
71

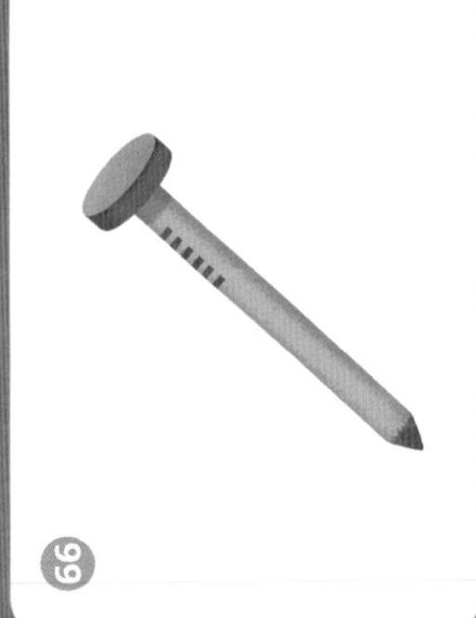
66
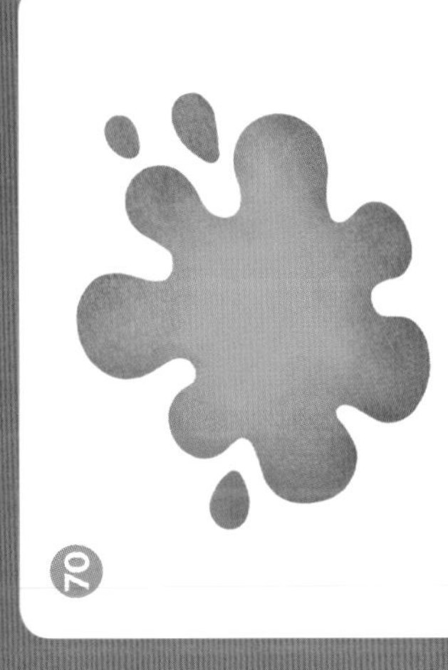
70

65
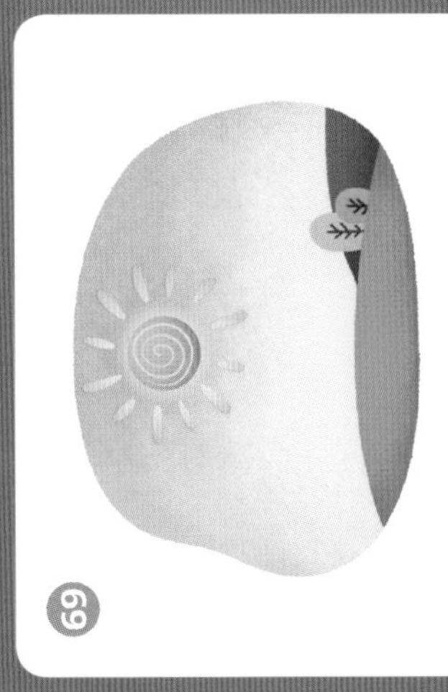
69

train	rain	nail	mail
tray	hay	gray	day

Congratulations!

Let's Go to the English World

Phonics 3 Long Vowels

The certificate is presented to

________________________.

Best

________________ Date

________________ Signature

Sticker Chart

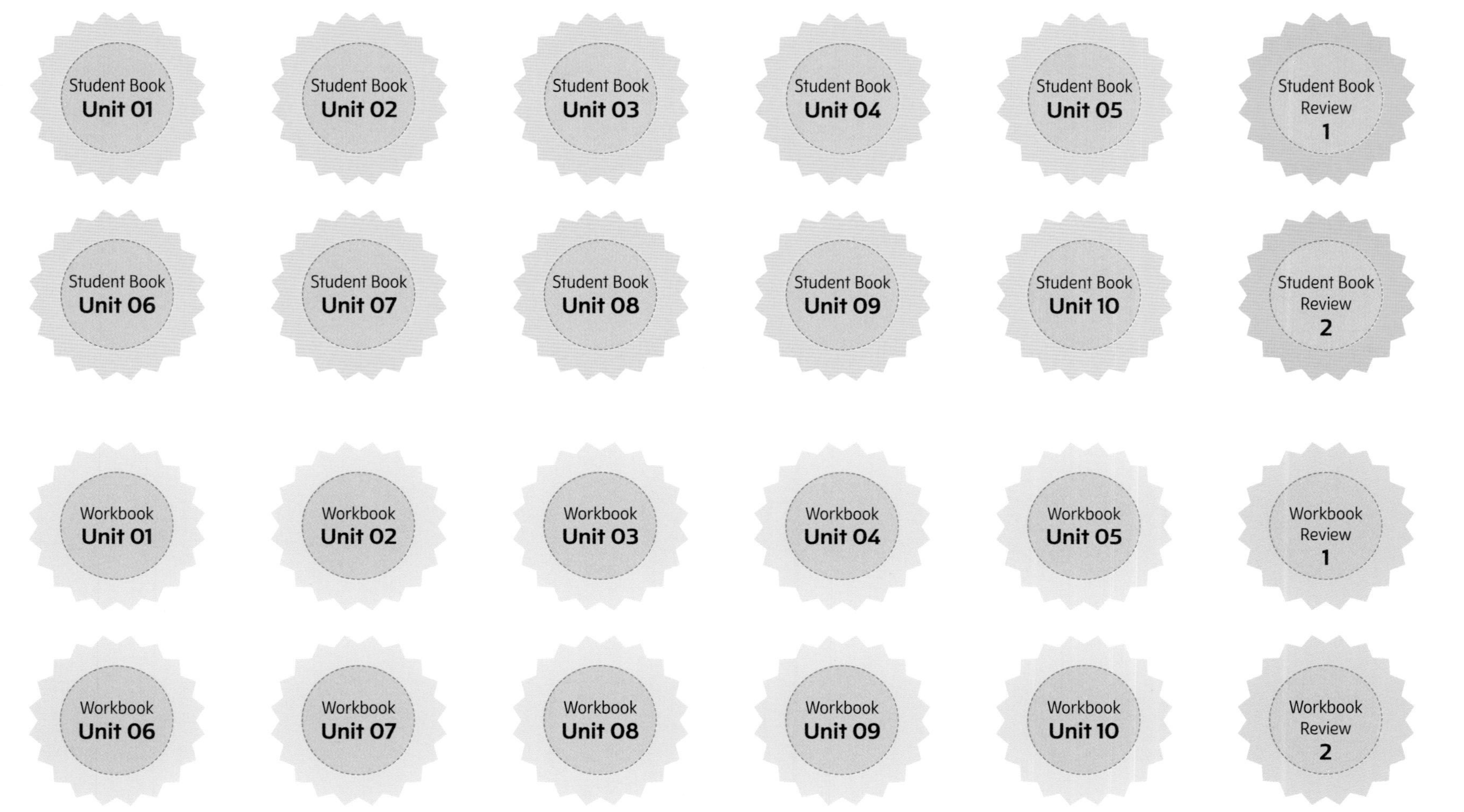

Student Book Unit 01
Student Book Unit 02
Student Book Unit 03
Student Book Unit 04
Student Book Unit 05
Student Book Review 1
Student Book Unit 06
Student Book Unit 07
Student Book Unit 08
Student Book Unit 09
Student Book Unit 10
Student Book Review 2
Workbook Unit 01
Workbook Unit 02
Workbook Unit 03
Workbook Unit 04
Workbook Unit 05
Workbook Review 1
Workbook Unit 06
Workbook Unit 07
Workbook Unit 08
Workbook Unit 09
Workbook Unit 10
Workbook Review 2

Unit 01 p. 8

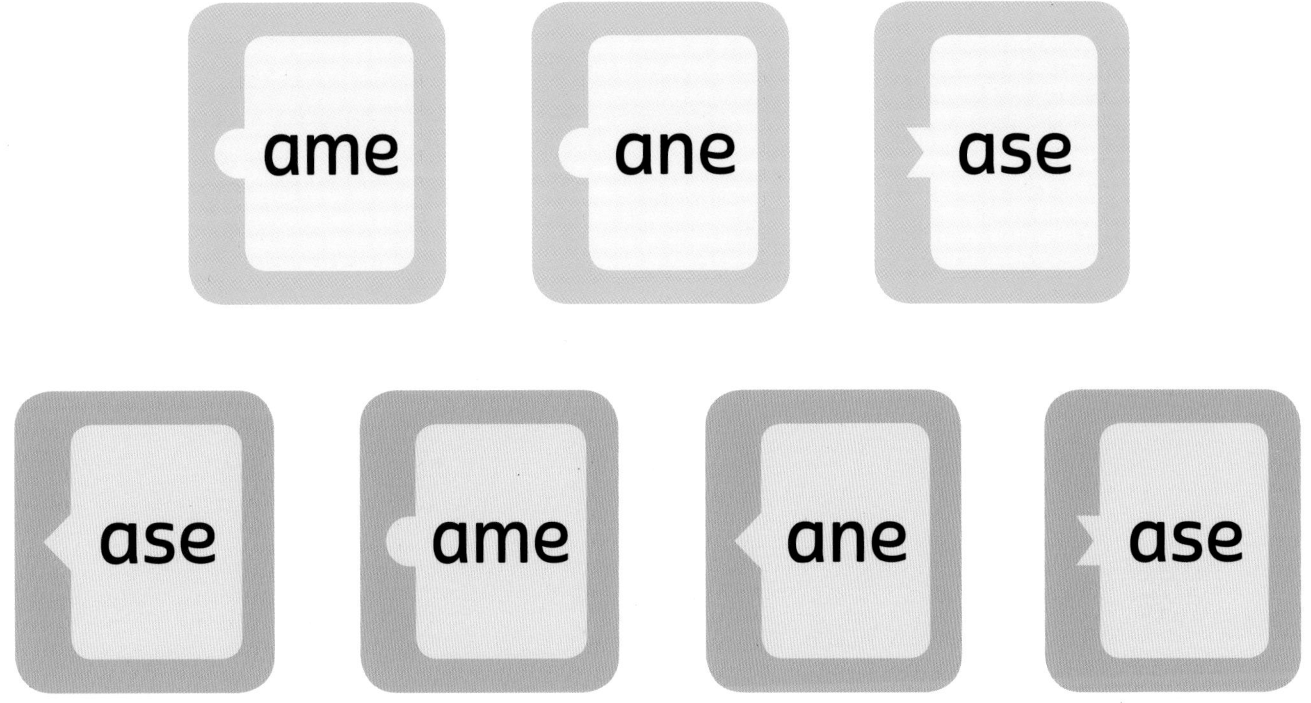
ame
ane
ase
ase
ame
ane
ase

Unit 03 p. 24

ike
ime
ine
ine
ime
ike
ine

Unit 05 p. 40

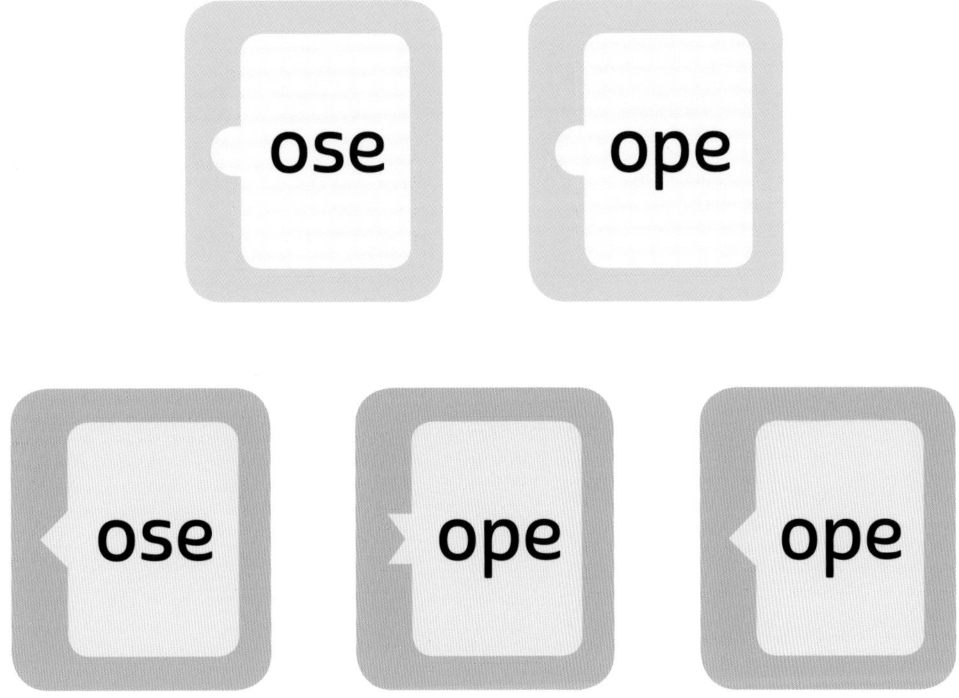
ose
ope
ose
ope
ope

Unit 07 p. 60

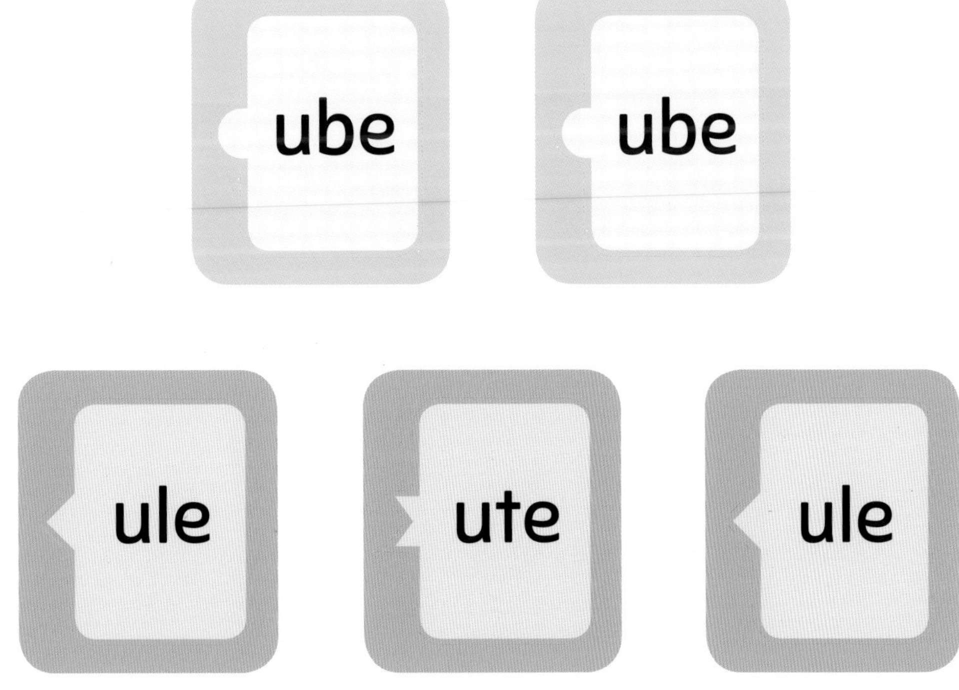
ube
ube
ule
ute
ule

Praise Stickers

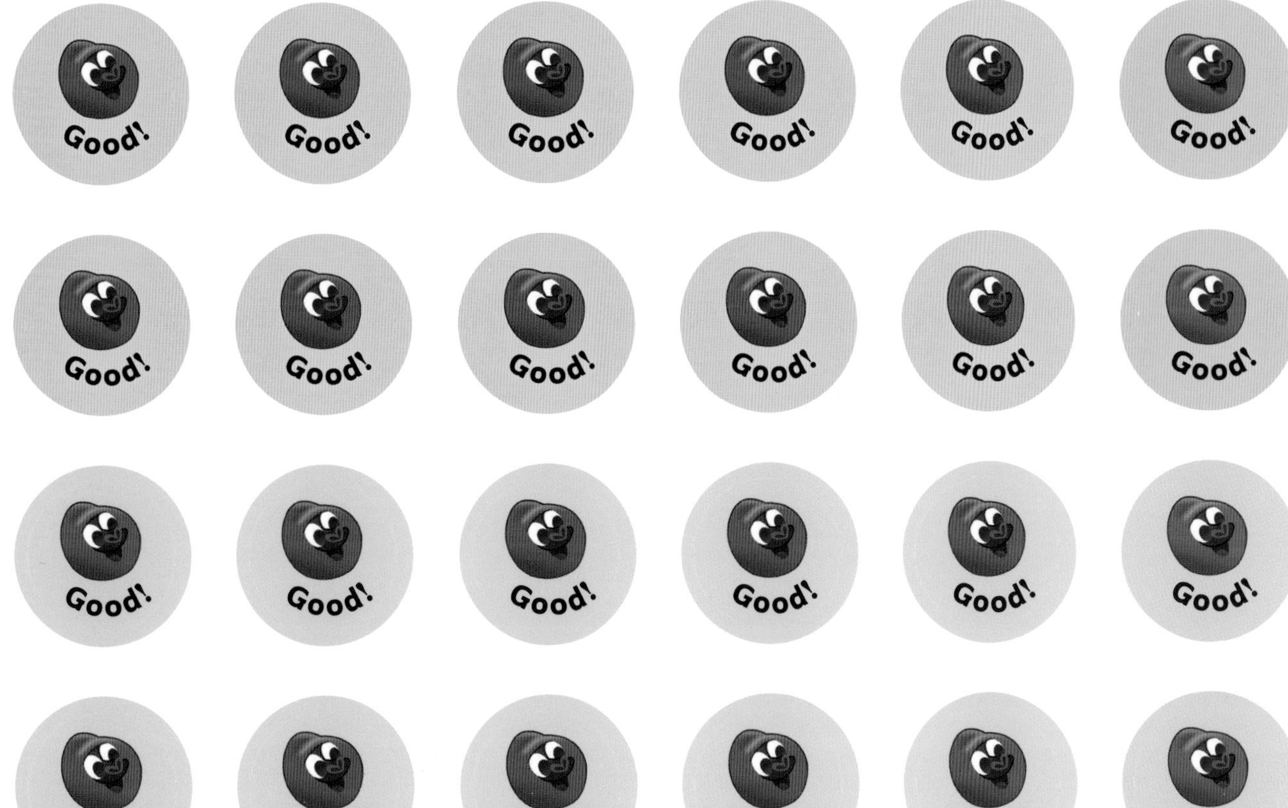
Good!
Good!
Good!
Good!
Good!
Good!
Good!
Good!
Good!
Good!
Good!
Good!
Good!
Good!
Good!
Good!
Good!
Good!
Good!
Good!
Good!
Good!
Good!
Good!

LET'S GO
2nd Edition
to the English World
3

WORKBOOK

Phonics

Long Vowels

CHUNJAE EDUCATION, INC.

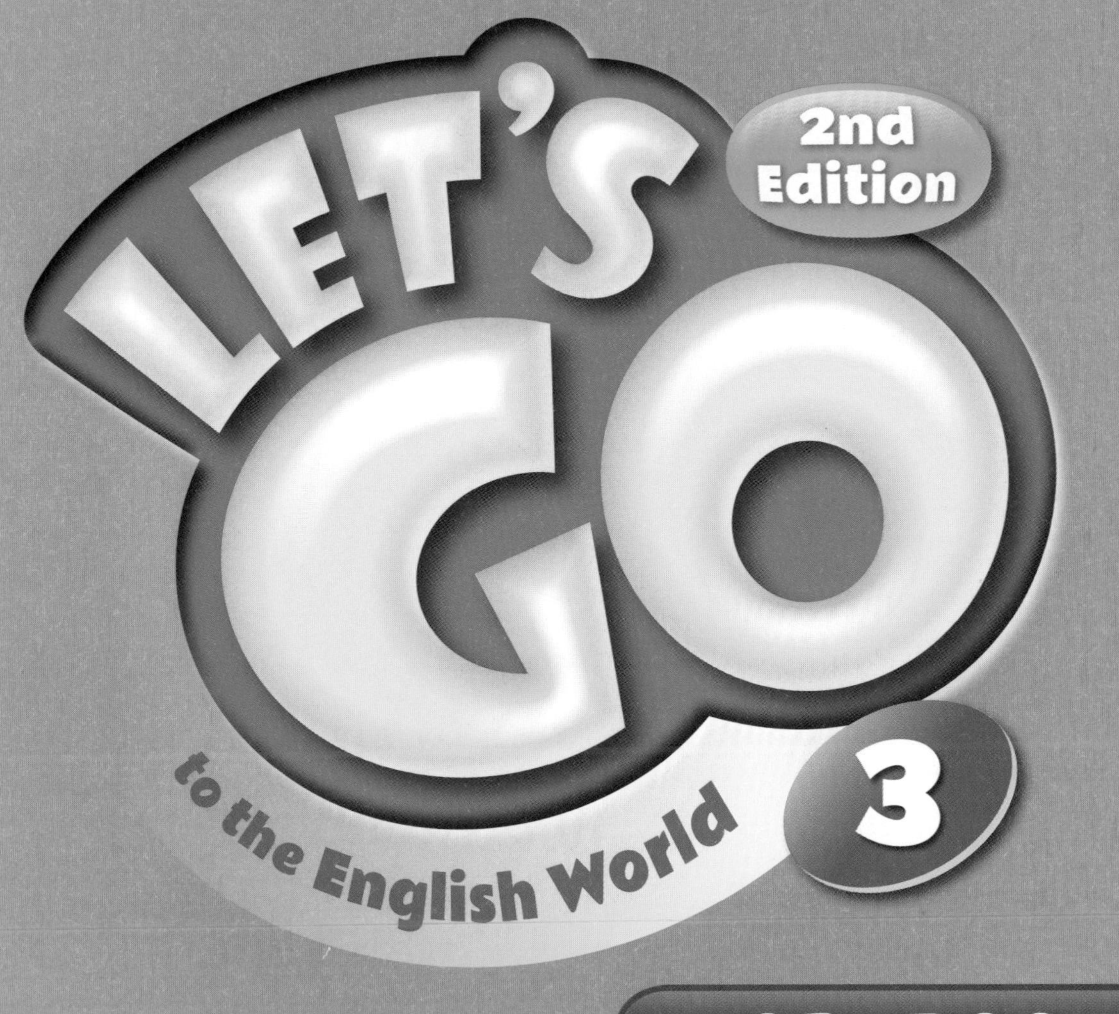
LET'S
2nd Edition
GO
to the English World
3

WORKBOOK

Phonics

Long Vowels

CHUNJAE EDUCATION, INC.

Unit 01 Long Vowel a

A Choose and match.

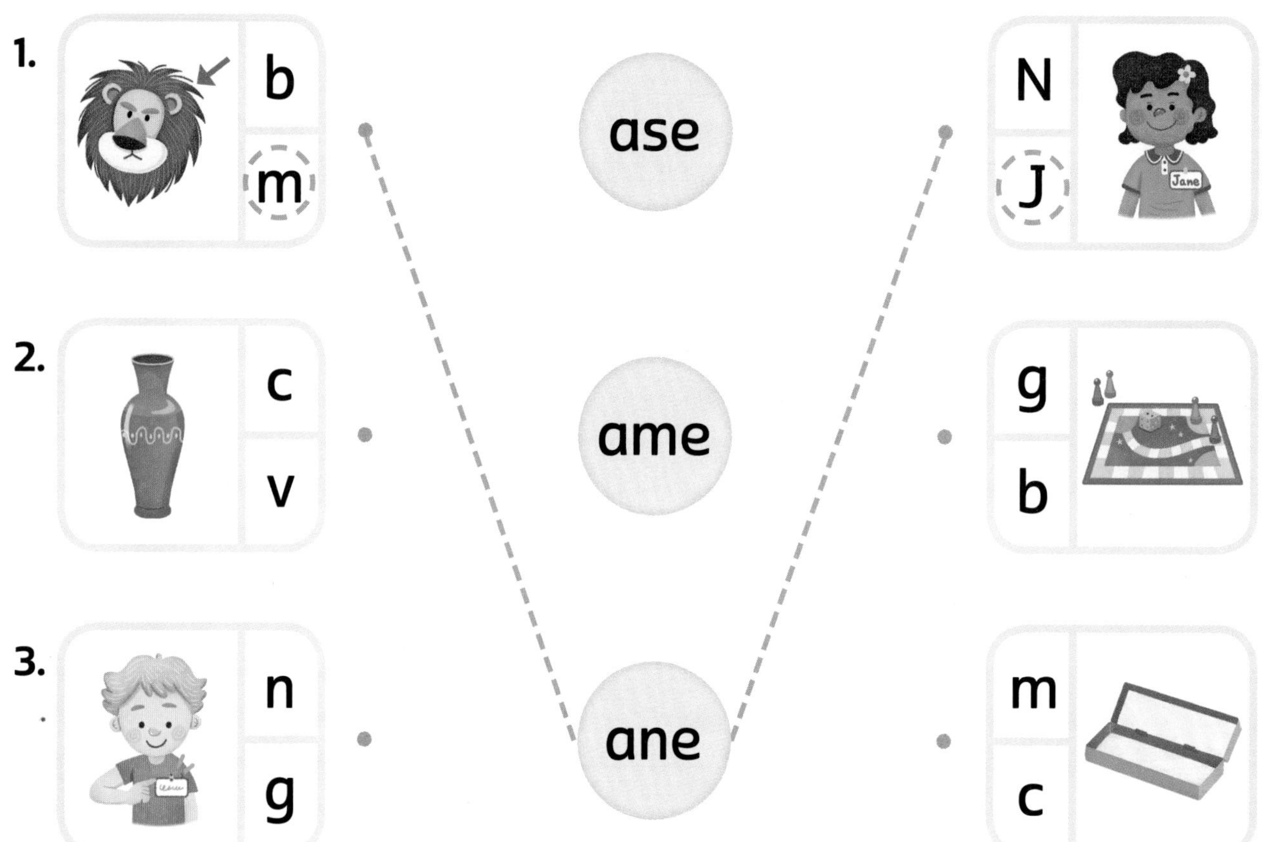
1.
b
m
2.
c
v
3.
n
g
ase
ame
ane
N
J
Jane
g
b
m
c

B Read and circle.

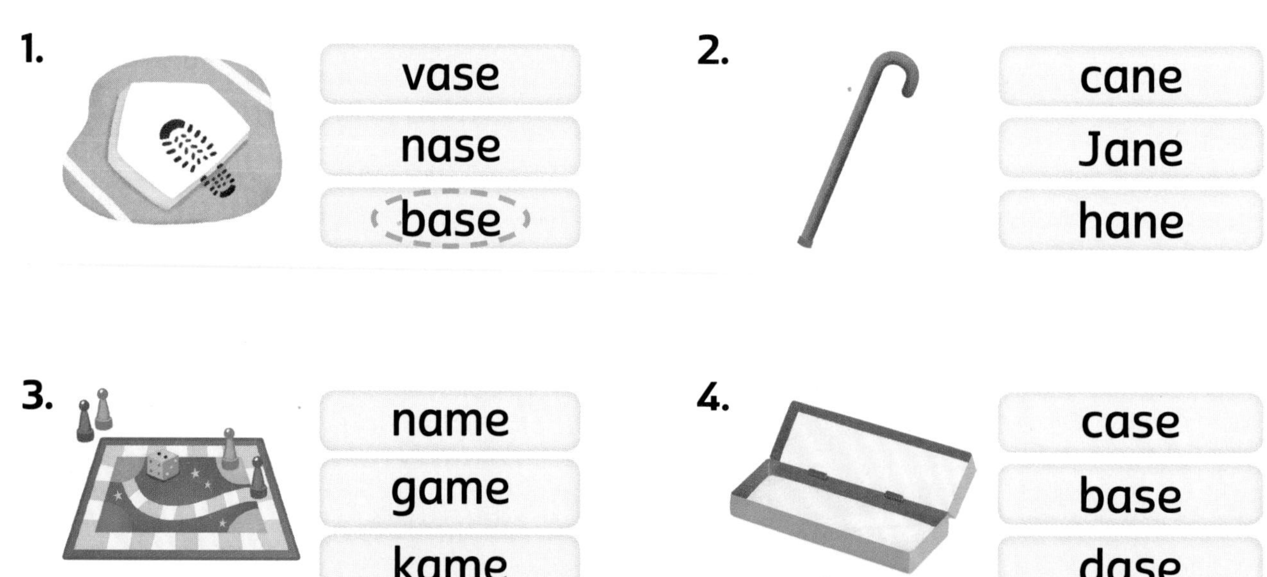
1.
vase
nase
base
2.
cane
Jane
hane
3.
name
game
kame
4.
case
base
dase

C Say and choose.

1. ame

2. ane

Jane
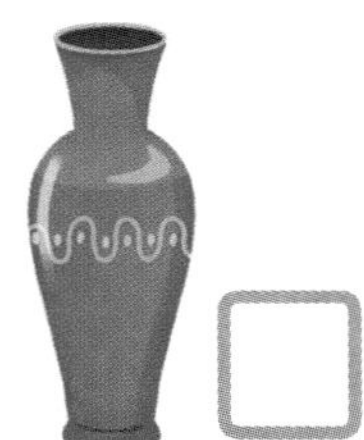
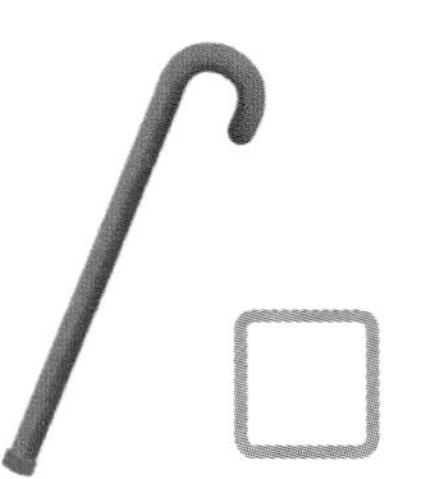

3. ase

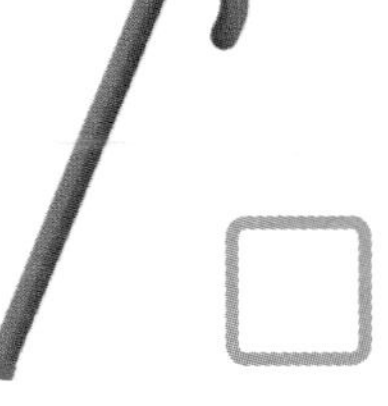
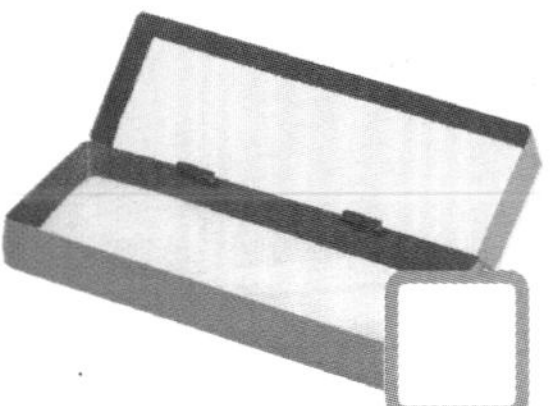

D Unscramble and write.

1. 

a v e s

vase

2. 

m e n a

3. 

e n m a

E Choose and write.

ame　　ane　　ase

1. 
Jane

Jane

2. 

c

3. 

n

4. 

v

5. 

g

6. 

c

7. 

m

8. 

b

F Read and number.

1 

2 
TED

3 

1. A lion with a mane is on the base. [3]
2. My name is on the cane. [ ]
3. A vase is in the case. [ ]

G Read and trace.

1. My name is on the cane.

2.  A lion with a mane is on the base.

3. 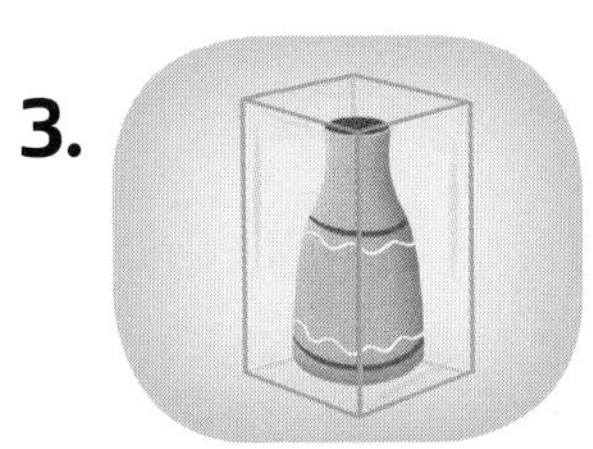 A vase is in the case.

Unit 02 Long Vowel a

A Choose and match.

1. 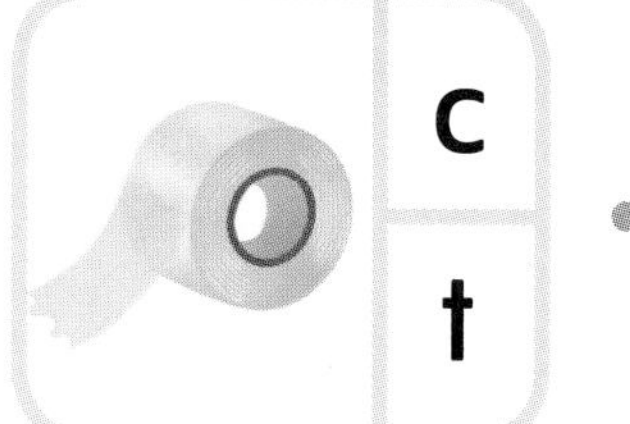 c / t • ave • l / w 

2. 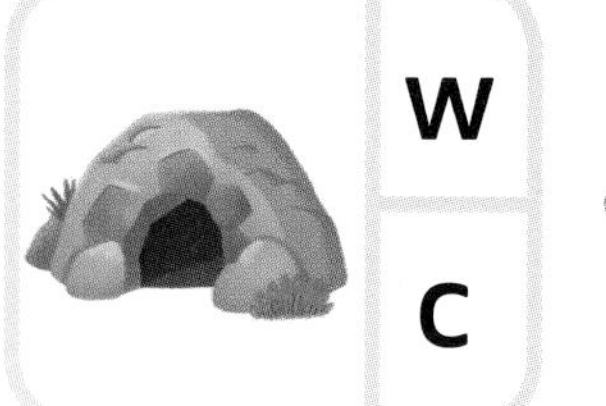 w / c • ape • t / l 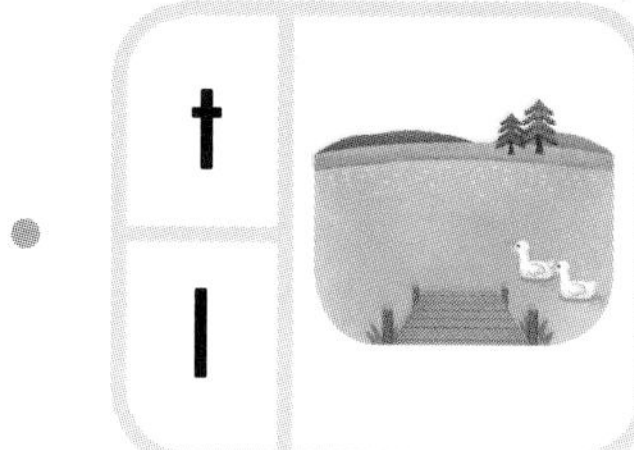

3.  b / l • ake • c / b

B Read and circle.

1. 
   - bake
   - cake
   - dake

2. 
   - rave
   - cave
   - wave

3. 
   - cape
   - jape
   - tape

4. 
   - lake
   - wake
   - kake

C Say and choose.

1\. ake

2\. ape

3\. ave

D Unscramble and write.

1\. 

e w k a

2\. 

v a e c

3\. 

p t e a

E Choose and write.

ake　　ape　　ave

1. 

c

2. 

l

3. 

c

4.

w

5. 

t

6. 

c

7. 

w

8. 

b

F Read and number.

1

2

3

1. Ben has a cape and tape. ☐
2. I see a cave by the lake. ☐
3. We bake a cake. ☐

G Read and trace.

1.

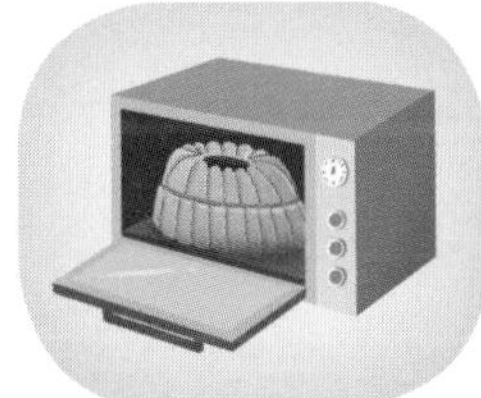

We bake a cake.

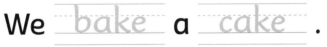

2.

I see a cave by the lake.

3.

Ben has a cape and tape.

Unit 03 Long Vowel i

A Choose and match.

1.  t / n • ime • b / h 

2.  v / h • ine • v / p 

3. 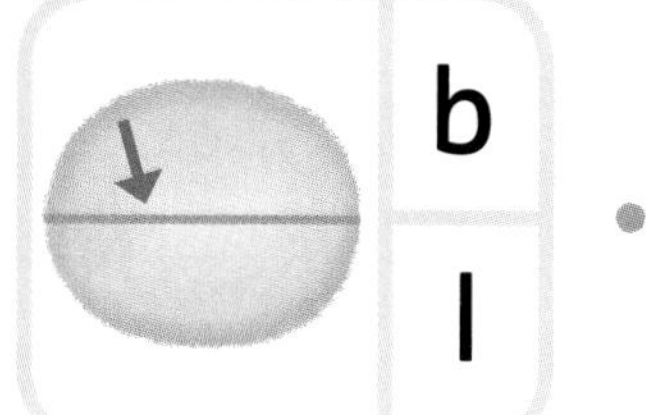 b / l • ike • l / t

B Read and circle.

1. 
   - line
   - rine
   - nine

2. 
   - hike
   - fike
   - bike

3. 
   - vime
   - lime
   - time

4. 
   - nine
   - kine
   - vine

C Say and choose.

1. ike

2. ime

02:30

3. ine

D Unscramble and write.

1. 
02:30

i m e t

____

2. 

k i b e

____

3. 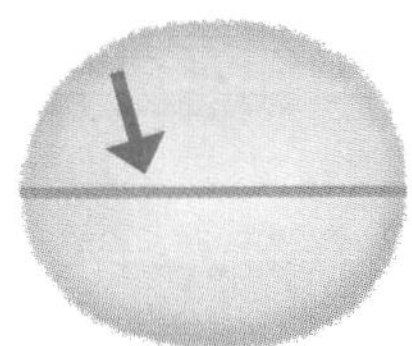

i l n e

____

E Choose and write.

ike　　ime　　ine

1. 

n

2. 

h

3. 

l

4. 

l

5. 

b

6. 

v

7. 
02:30

t

8. 

p

F Read and number.

1
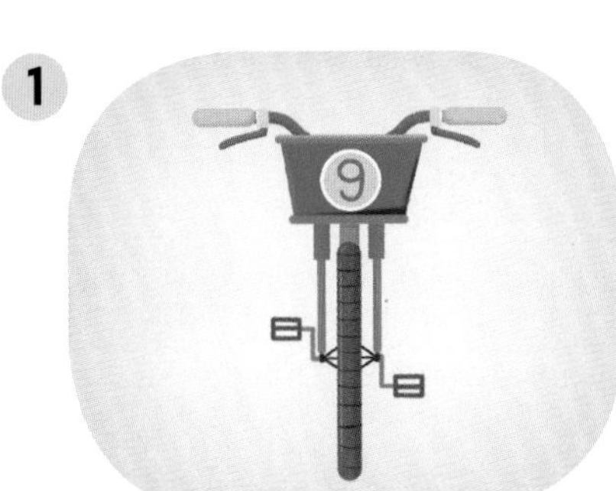
9

2

3

1. They hike up to the pine.
2. There is a lime on the line.
3. A nine is on the bike.

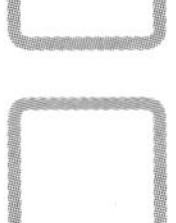

G Read and trace.

1. 

They hike up to the pine.

2. 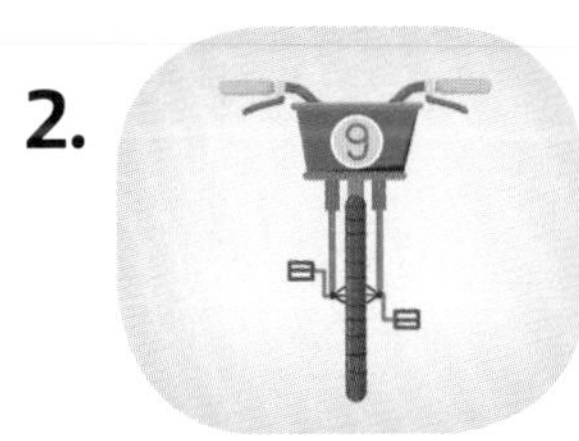
9

A nine is on the bike.

3. 

There is a lime on the line.

Unit
04

Long Vowel i

A Choose and match.

1. 

h / j • ive • k / c

2. 

p / b • ide • l / r

3. 

d / b • ite • k / h

B Read and circle.

1. 

five
hive
mive

2. 

ride
side
dide

3. 

hive
dive
tive

4. 

fite
bite
kite

C Say and choose.

1.

ide

2.

ite

3.

ive

D Unscramble and write.

1.
i b e t
2.
v e d i
3.
e i d r

E Choose and write.

ide | ite | ive

1. 

h

2.

d

3. 

r

4. 

k

5. 

b

6. 

f

7. 

h

8. 

s

F Read and number.

1 
2 
3 

1. Five ants dive into the water. ☐
2. A bee can hide in a hive. ☐
3. The cat likes to bite a kite. ☐

G Read and trace.

1. 
The cat likes to bite a kite.

2. 
A bee can hide in a hive.

3. 
Five ants dive into the water.

Unit 05

Long Vowel O

A Choose and match.

1.  h / j

2. p / b 

ope

3.  m / n

4. h / f 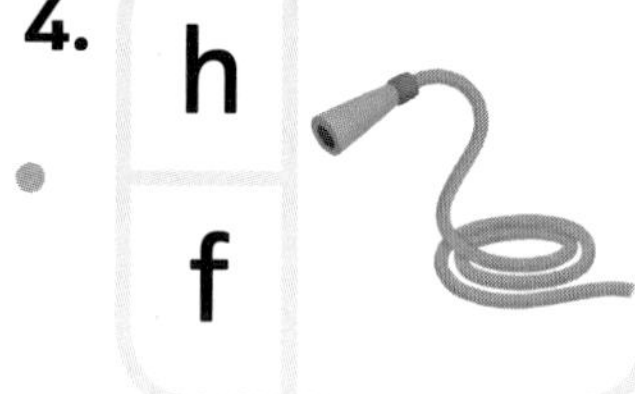

ose

5.  r / t

6. l / r 

B Read and circle.

1. 
   - rose
   - nose
   - mose

2. 
   - kose
   - rose
   - hose

3. 
   - lope
   - hope
   - rope

4. 
   - hope
   - cope
   - pope

C Say and choose.

1\. ope

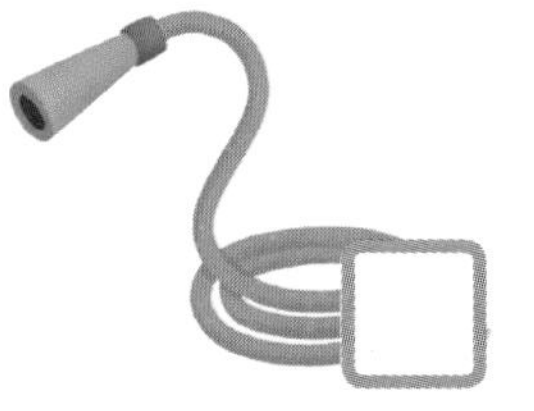

2\. ose

D Unscramble and write.

1\. 

o p e h

2\. 

p e o p

3\. 

e o s r

4\. s h e o

E Choose and write.

ope　　ose

1. 

h

2. 

r

3. 

p

4. 

h

5.

r

6. 

n

F Read and number.

1 
2 
3 

1. I hope to meet the pope. ☐
2. The dog's nose smells a rose. ☐
3. She has a rope and a hose. ☐

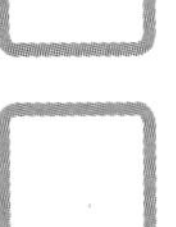

G Read and trace.

1. The dog's nose smells a rose.

2. She has a rope and a hose.

3. I hope to meet the pope.

Review 1

A Look and circle.

1. ave

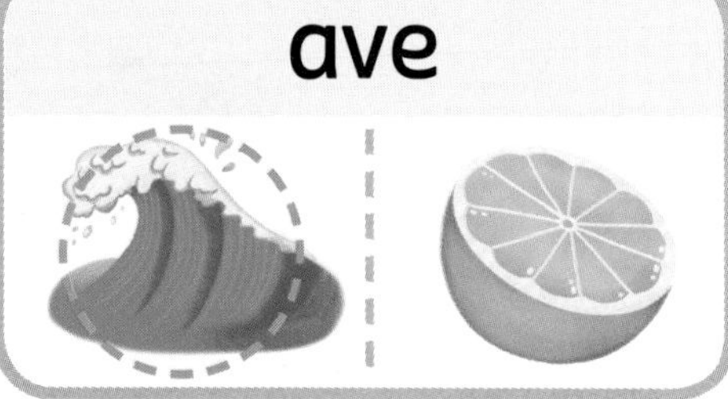

2. ane

3. ope

4. ite

5. ape

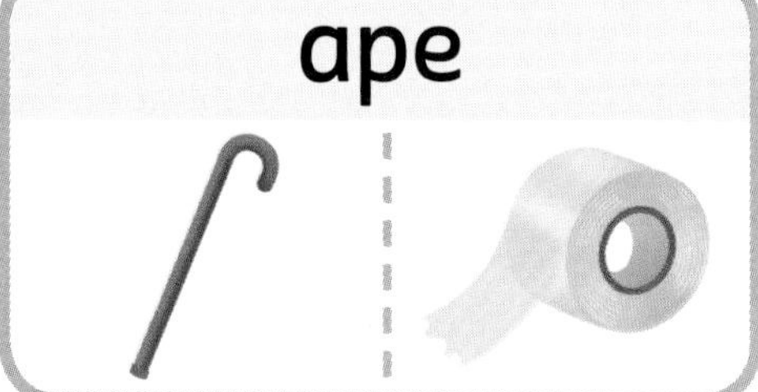

6. ime

02:30

B Write and say.

1. 

p_o_p_e

2. 

hi____

3. 

l__n__

4. 

b____e

5. 

ga____

6. 
Jane

J____e

C Look and write.

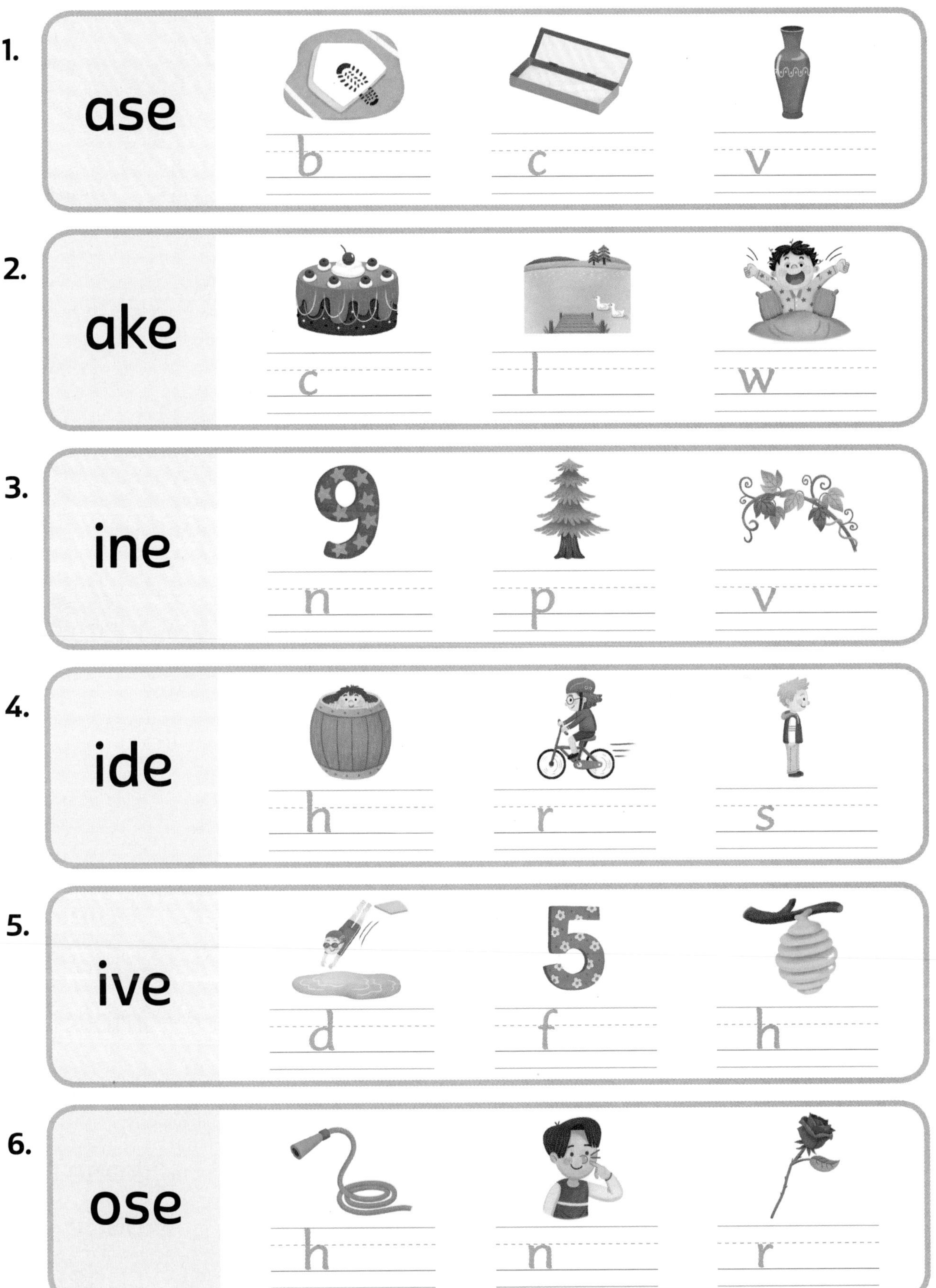
1.
ase
b
c
v
2.
ake
c
l
w
3.
ine
9
n
p
v
4.
ide
h
r
s
5.
ive
d
5
f
h
6.
ose
h
n
r

Unit 06

Long Vowel O

A Choose and match.

1. 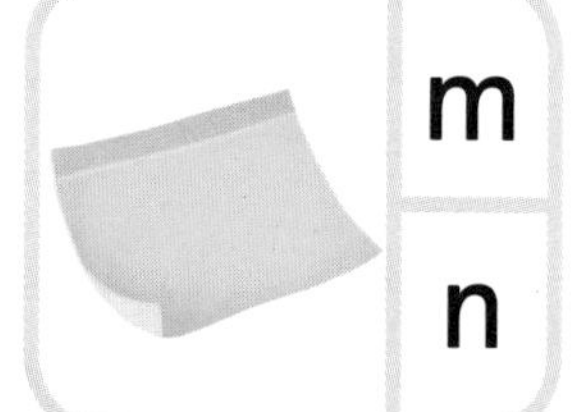

m / n • ole • c / k

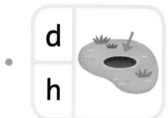

2. 

m / l • ote • d / h

3. 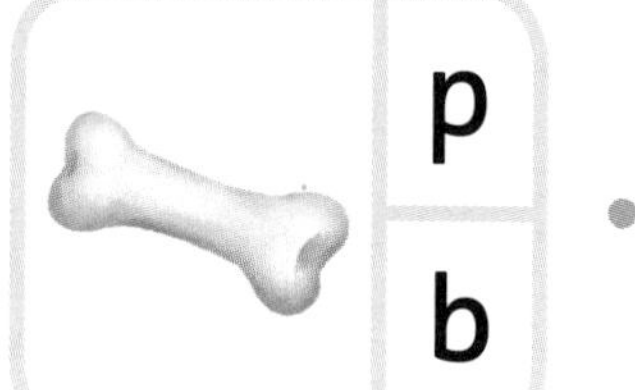

p / b • one • v / f 

B Read and circle.

1. 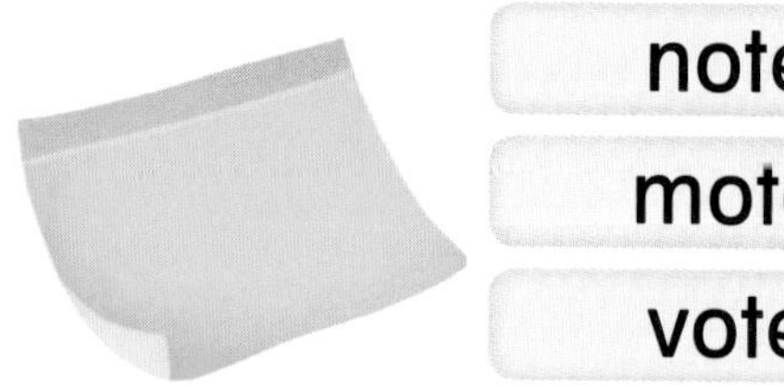

note
mote
vote

2. 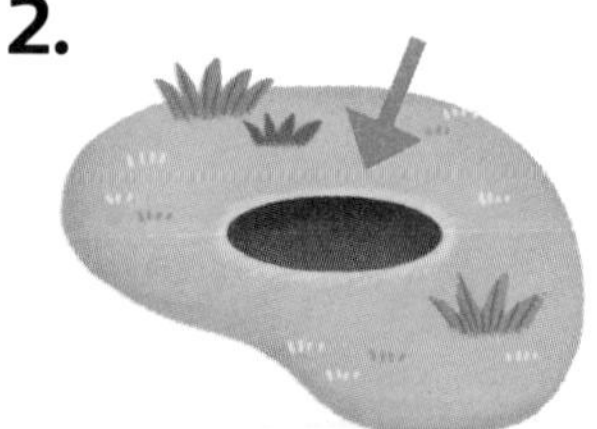

hole
tole
mole

3. 

wole
mole
hole

4. 

kone
bone
cone

C Say and choose.

1.

ole

2.
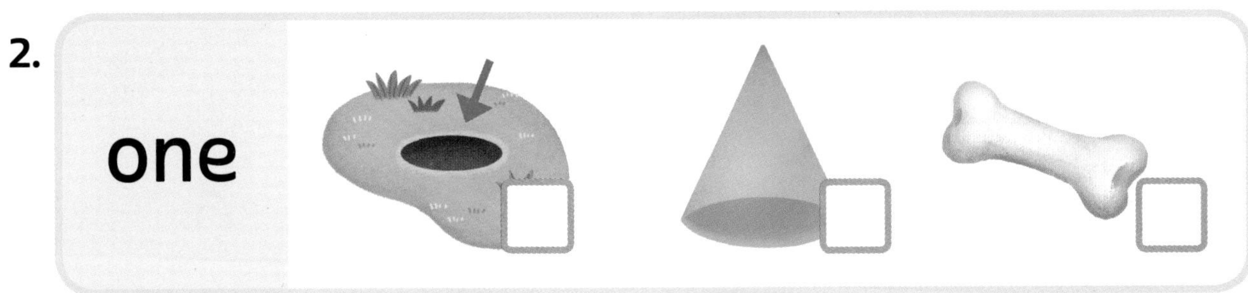
one

3.
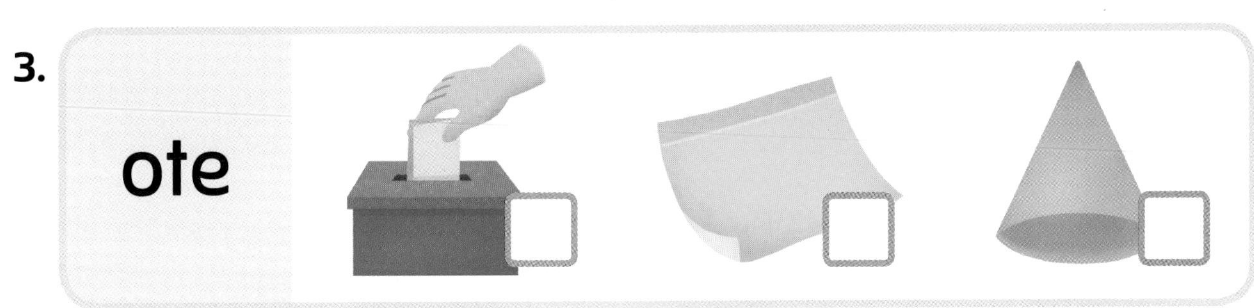
ote

D Unscramble and write.

1.
b n e o
2.
o e h l
3.
e v o t

E Choose and write.

ole one ote

1. 

c

2. 

n

3. 

h

4. 

v

5. 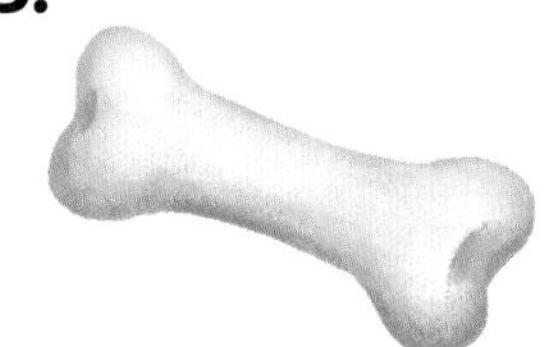

b

6. 

m

F Read and number.

1 

2 

3 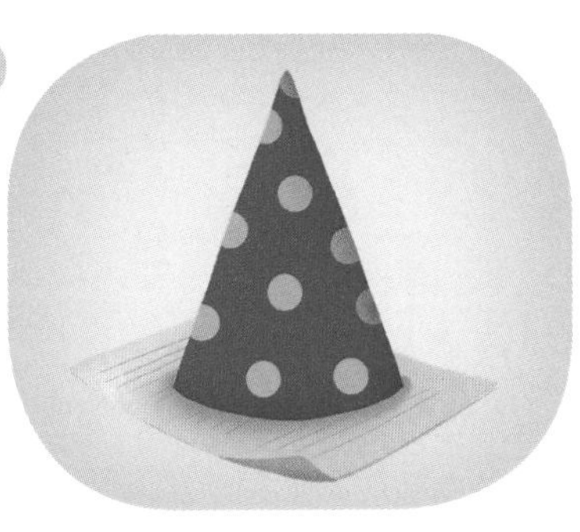

1. The mole wants to vote. ☐
2. A note is under the cone. ☐
3. A dog sees a bone in a hole. ☐

G Read and trace.

1. 

A note is under the cone.

2. 

A dog sees a bone in a hole.

3. 

The mole wants to vote.

Unit 07

Long Vowel U

A Choose and match.

1.

s
r

ule

c
k

2.

c
s

ube

n
m

3.

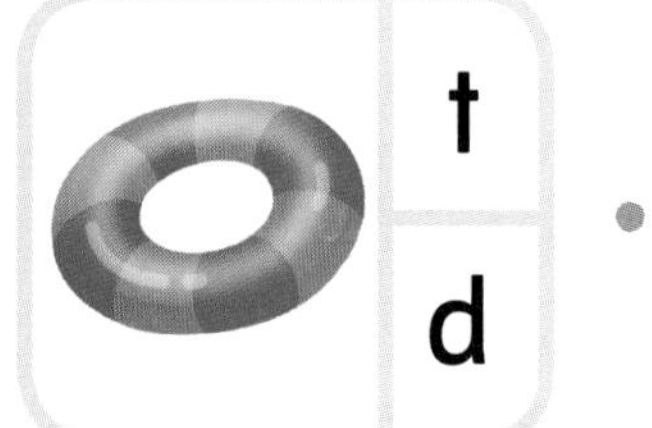

t
d

ute

l
m

B Read and circle.

1.

rule
mule
kule

2.

pube
cube
tube

3.

tute
cute
mute

4.

rule
dule
mule

C Say and choose.

1. ube

2. ule

3. ute

D Unscramble and write.

1. 

u t e b

2. 

u m e l

3. 

m e u t

E Choose and write.

ube ule ute

1. 

m

2. 

t

3.

m

4. 

r

5. 

c

6. 

c

F Read and number.

1 

2 

3 

1. A cute doll is in the cube. ☐
2. Keep the rules to use the tube. ☐
3. The mule is mute. ☐

G Read and trace.

1. 

The mule is mute.

2. 

A cute doll is in the cube.

3. 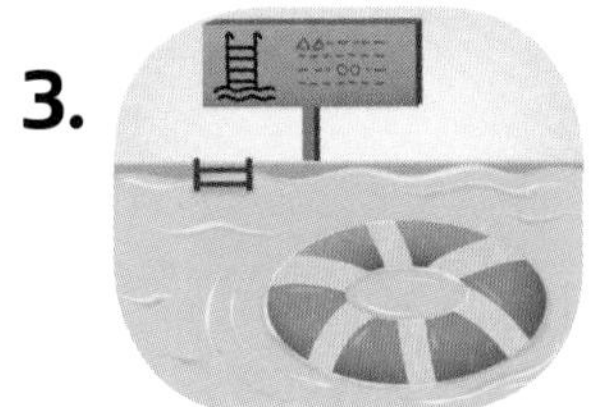

Keep the rules to use the tube.

Unit 08 Long Vowel U

A Choose and match.

1. 

t
b

use

2.
m
f

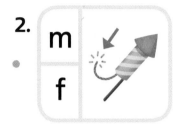

uge

3. 

s
h

une

4.
d
l

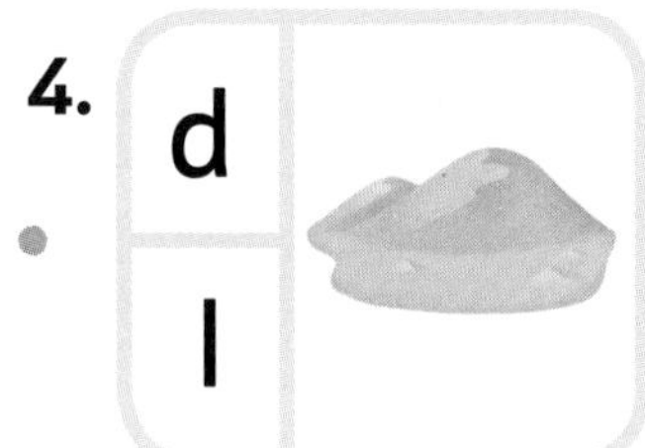

B Read and circle.

1. 
6

June
cune
dune

2.

luge
kuge
huge

3. 

fuse
duse
use

4.

June
tune
fune

C Say and choose.

1. une

2. use

D Unscramble and write.

1. 

s u f e

2. 

u e J n

3. 

e h g u

4. 

n u e d

E Choose and write.

uge | une | use

1. 

use

2. 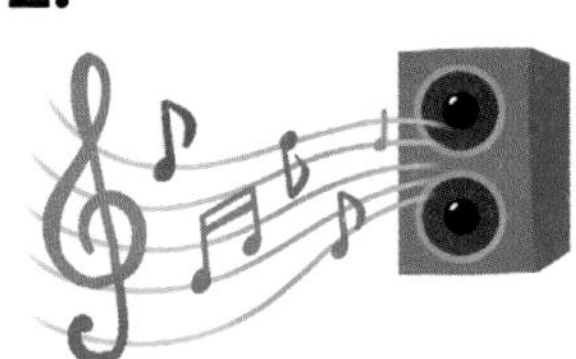

t

3. h

4. 
6

J

5. 

f

6. 

d

F Read and number.

1 
2 
6
3 

1. A huge bear has a fuse. ☐
2. I use a fan in June. ☐
3. I dance to a tune on the dune. ☐

G Read and trace.

1.  I dance to a tune on the dune.

2. A huge bear has a fuse.

3.  I use a fan in June.

Unit 09 Long Vowel ea, ee

A Choose and match.

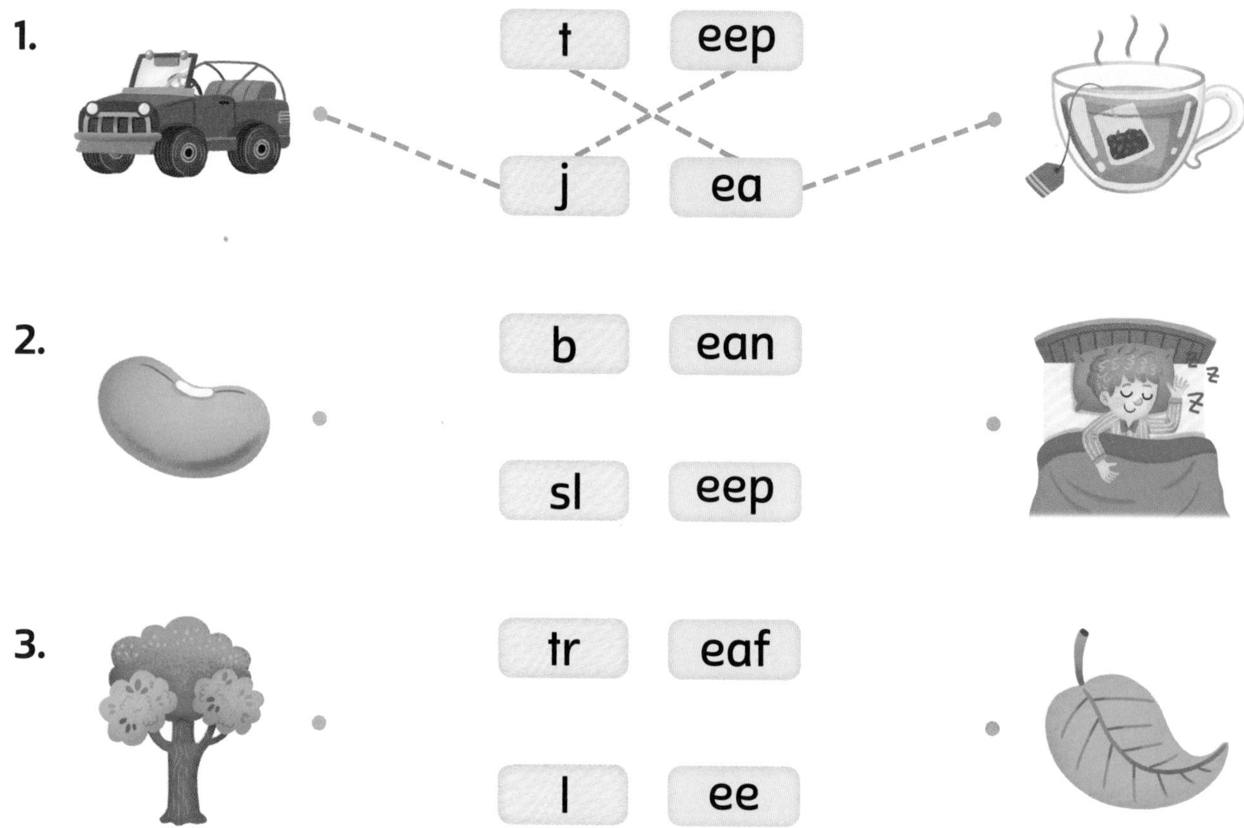

1.
t
eep
j
ea
2.
b
ean
sl
eep
3.
tr
eaf
l
ee

B Read and circle.

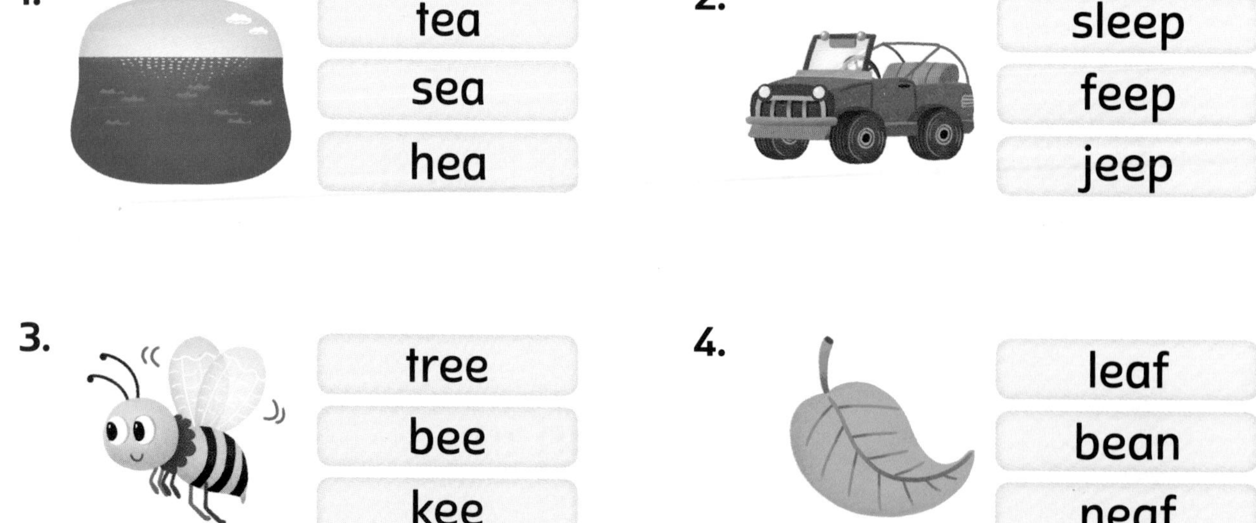

1.
tea
sea
hea
2.
sleep
feep
jeep
3.
tree
bee
kee
4.
leaf
bean
neaf

C Say and choose.

1.
ea
2.
ee

D Unscramble and write.

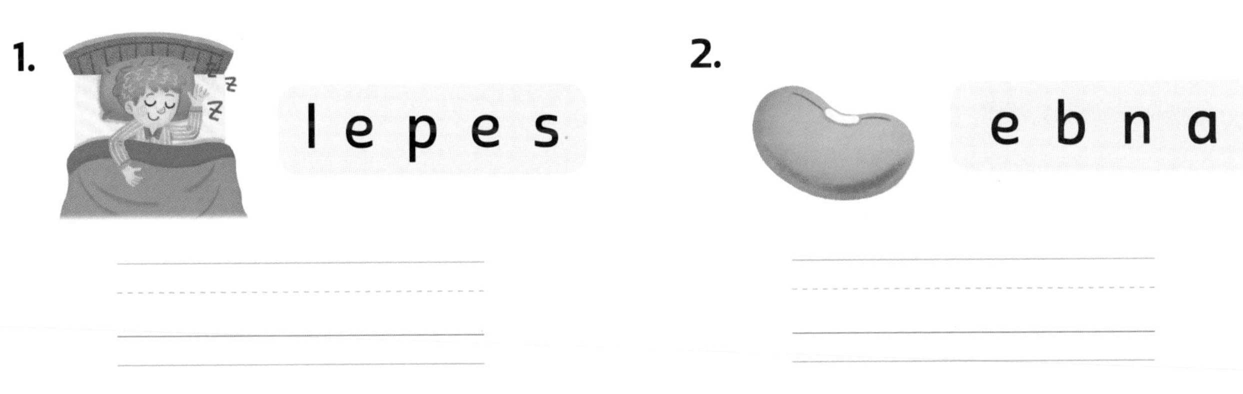
1.
l e p e s
2.
e b n a

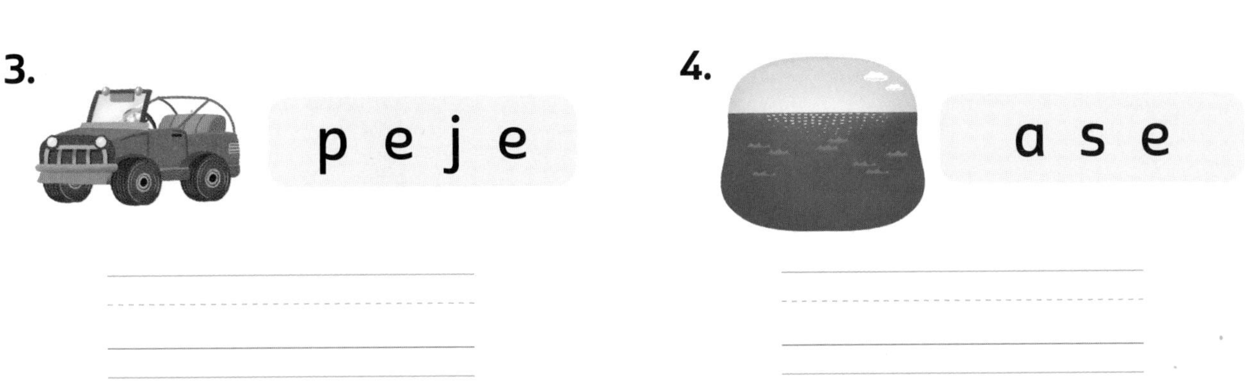
3.
p e j e
4.
a s e

E Choose and write.

ea　　ee

1.

s

2.

j p

3.

l f

4.

sl p

5.

b

6.

t

7.

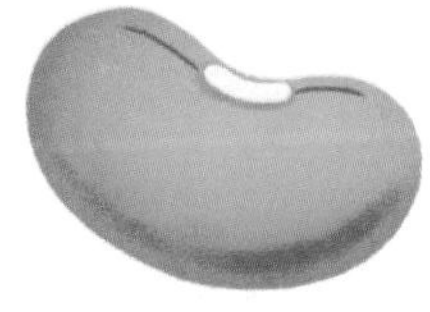

b n

8.

tr

F Read and number.

1 
2 
3 

1. A bee is on the leaf. ☐
2. I drink tea by the tree. ☐
3. The dogs sleep in the jeep. ☐

G Read and trace.

1. 
I drink tea by the tree.

2. 
A bee is on the leaf.

3. 
The dogs sleep in the jeep.

Unit 10

Long Vowel ai, ay

A Choose and match.

1. 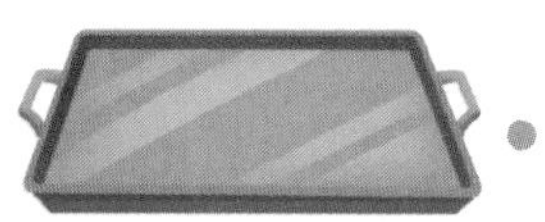

tr	ay
m	ail

2. 

h	ain
tr	ay

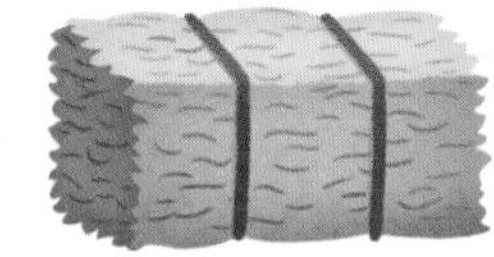

3. 

n	ail
d	ay

B Read and circle.

1. 

cail
mail
nail

2. 

cray
day
gray

3. 

hain
train
rain

4. 

day
vay
hay

C Say and choose.

1. ai

2. ay

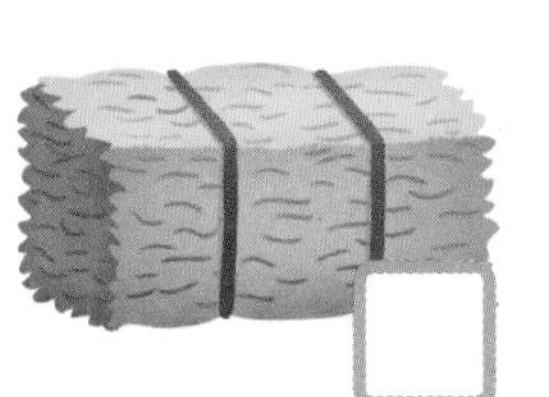

D Unscramble and write.

1. 

r i n a

2. 

a r g y

3. 

l i m a

4. 

i a l n

E Choose and write.

ai   ay

1. 

m __ l

2. 

gr __

3. 

d __

4. 

tr __ n

5. 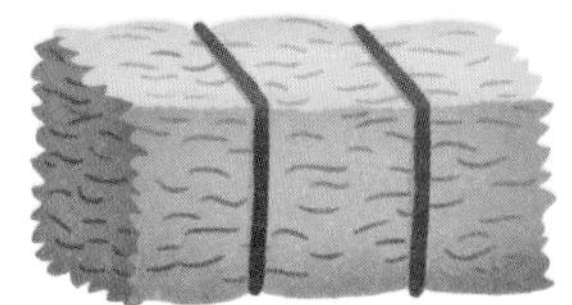

h __

6. 

r __ n

7. 

tr __

8. 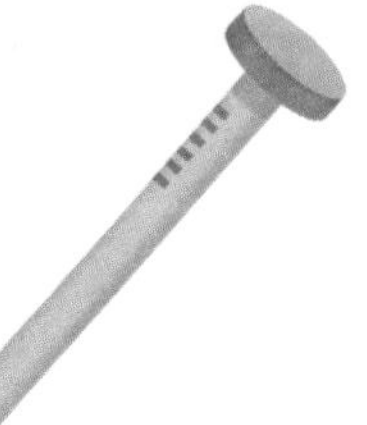

n __ l

F Read and number.

1 
2 
3 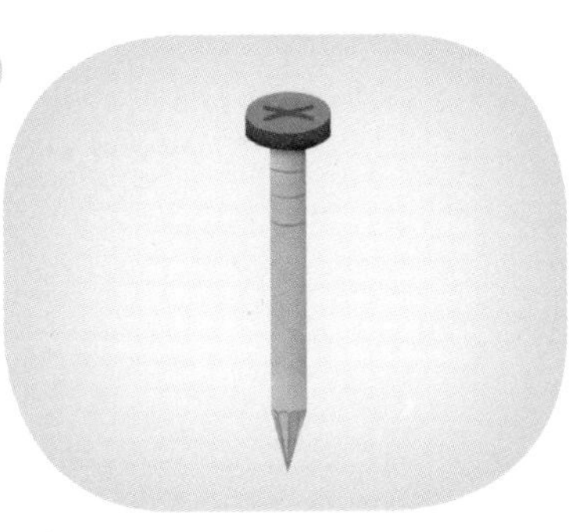

1. A train runs in the rain. ☐
2. Hay is on the tray. ☐
3. The nail is gray. ☐

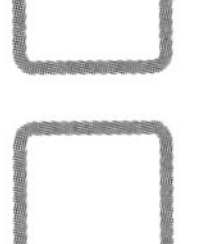

G Read and trace.

1. 
The nail is gray.

2. 
Hay is on the tray.

3. 
A train runs in the rain.

Review 2

A Look and circle.

1. ube

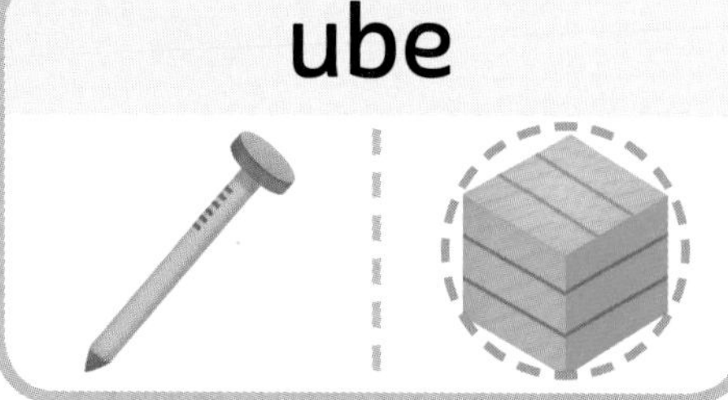

2. ee

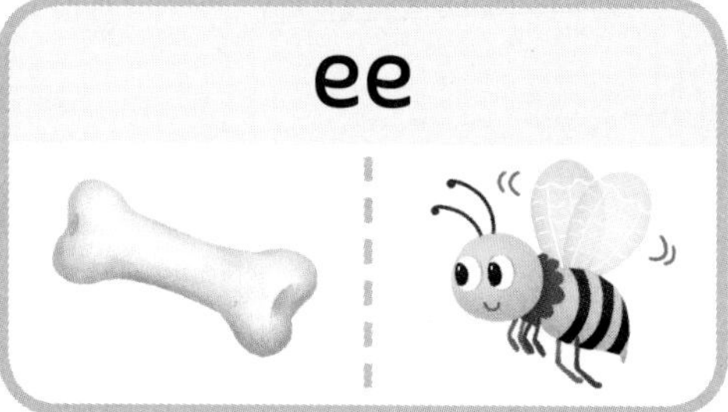

3. ote

4. use

5. ai

6. ule

B Write and say.

1. 

l_ea_f

2. 

h__g__

3. 

mu____

4. 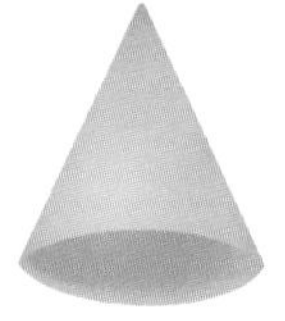

c__n__

5. 

____te

6. 

tr____n

C Look and write.

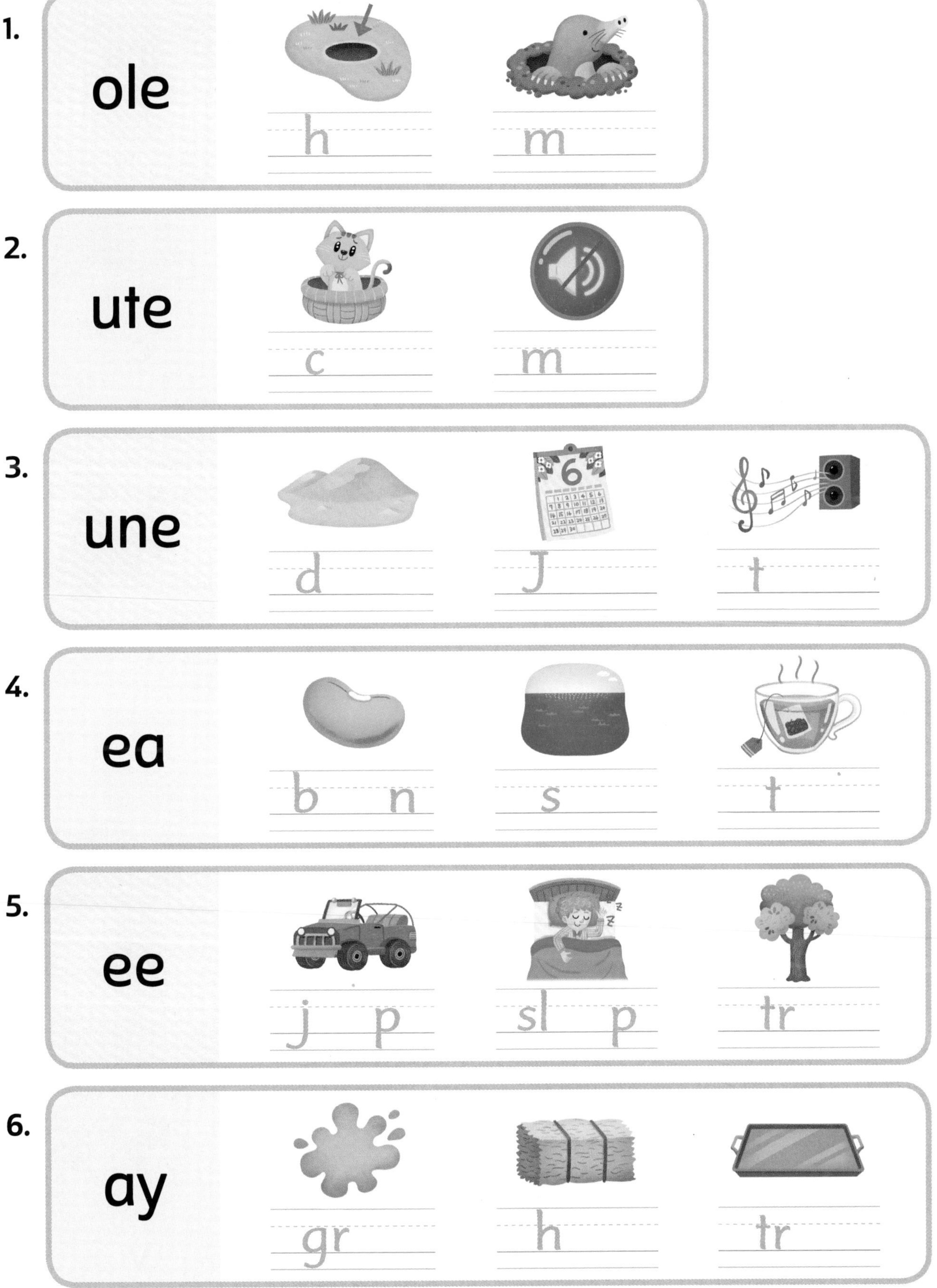
1.
ole
h
m
2.
ute
c
m
3.
une
d
J
t
4.
ea
b n
s
t
5.
ee
j p
sl p
tr
6.
ay
gr
h
tr

Final Review

Choose and write.

ame ase ake ape ave ike ine

wake

p

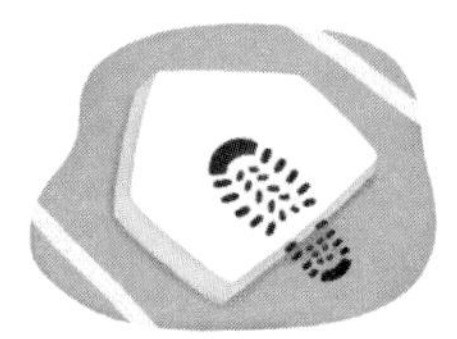
b

c

h

g

v

c

b

c

n

w

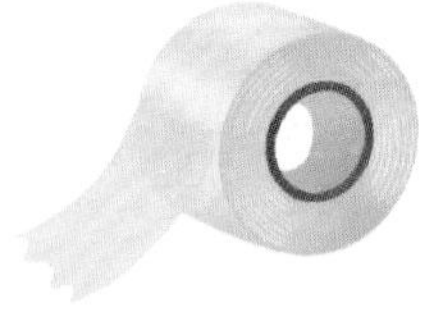
t

b

c

v

ite ive ope ose ole one ote

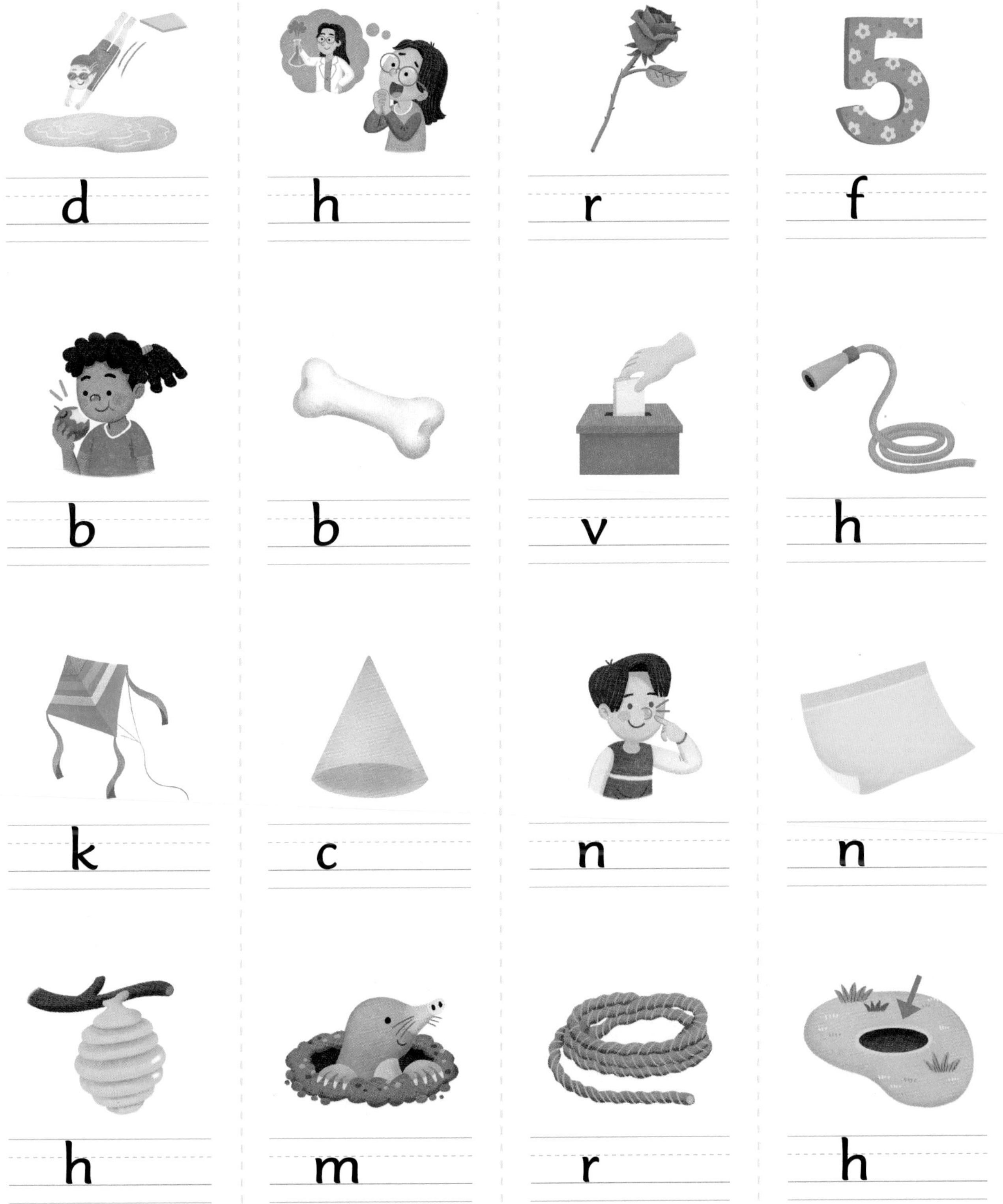

d
h
r
f
b
b
v
h
k
c
n
n
h
m
r
h

ube ute uge une ea ee ai

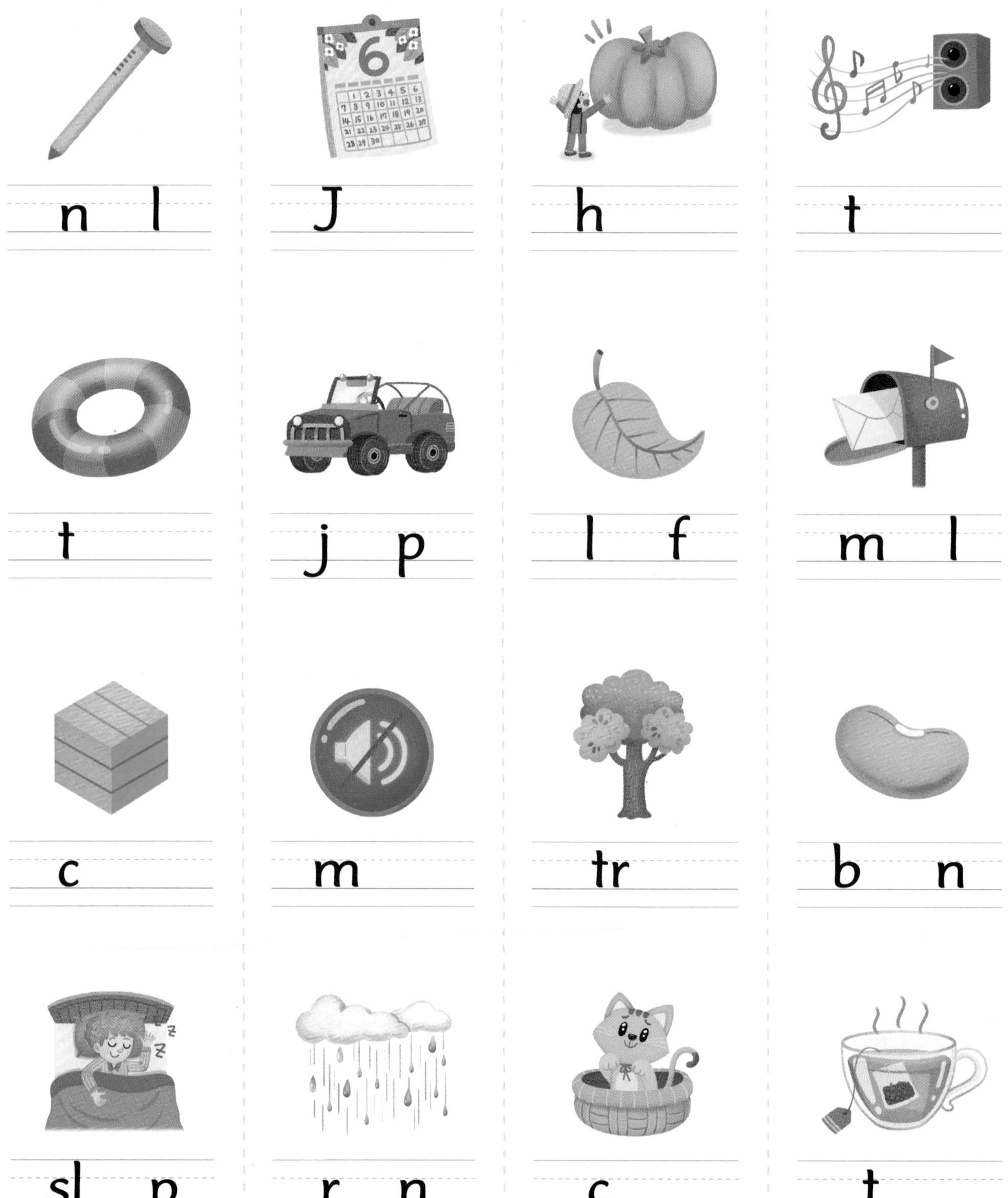
n l
J
h
t
t
j p
l f
m l
c
m
tr
b n
sl p
r n
c
t

2nd
Edition
LET'S
GO
to the English World
3
Phonics